How to
Succeed in Parenting:

120 Ways to Have a Great Family

by
Roberta Schultz Benor

PublishAmerica
Baltimore

First printing

ISBN: 1-4137-2806-5
PUBLISHED BY PUBLISHAMERICA, LLLP
www.publishamerica.com
Baltimore

Printed in the United States of America

To my parents, Estelle and Henry Schultz, who were my teachers.
To my children, Sarah, Miriam, and Aaron, who were my inspirations.
To my husband, David, who is my partner in love and parenting.

Acknowledgments

One Sunday evening my husband, David Benor, asked me what I planned to do the next day. Out burst the following sentence: "I am going to put my parenting class lectures into a book." I would like to thank him for his support of this project and of everything else I have done. Without him, I would not have our wonderful children, Sarah, Miriam, and Aaron, who inspired us to develop our own parenting skills. The delight and fulfillment that they bring us are beyond measure. My gratitude also goes to my parents, Estelle and Henry Schultz, who showed me by constant example how to have a loving family.

Thanks are due to Georgia Lewis of Montgomery County (Maryland) Public Schools, Adult Education Program, for exposing me to parenting classes and training me as an instructor, and to Toni Goodman, who hired me to teach parenting classes at the Jewish Community Center of Greater Washington. I would also like to thank the parents and children who took my classes for their encouragement. Special gratitude goes to Sandy Elson, for her years of friendship and for leading me to the talented illustrator, Jo-Anna McCort Fischman. I particularly appreciate Jo-Anna's ability to capture my themes in creative drawings. Finally, I am grateful to my extended family and friends for their support.

-Table of Contents-

-List of Games-

Definition of a Game: an activity which enlarges, changes, or elucidates a certain behavior, played to develop better relationships between family members.

Introduction

1) Adjustments

2) Early Socialization

3) Routines

4) Toilet Training

5) Nursery School

6) Discipline

7) Self-Esteem

8) Creativity

9) Children's Rights and Responsibilities

10) Sibling Rivalry

11) Parental Roles

12) The Grandparents
or the Grand Parents

13) Lemon-aid

Conclusion

Introduction

Introduction

I have perfect children. They have perfect tantrums, perfect sibling rivalry, and are perfectly obnoxious. It seems as though they have read ahead in the classic psychology textbooks and know how to behave at each step of the way. But they also are wonderful, thoughtful, considerate, and giving. The bottom line is that they are normal children doing what normal children are supposed to do– grow, develop, reach too far, come back for security, change moods, and blossom.

In this age of information, pregnant couples attend prepared childbirth classes and read and research to learn all they can about their pregnancies. However, we are never really prepared for the actual parenting that comes quickly on the heels of the arrival home from the hospital. My husband and I were not formally prepared, but we both came from warm, loving homes and approached our parenting jobs with an easygoing common sense. We followed my uncle's advice of remembering that babies bend before they break. We shared all the responsibilities we could. Also, we smiled so much at our babies that our cheeks often hurt by the end of the day.

We decided that we would try to remain pleasant as parents, although at times we almost forgot the meaning of the word. We read what all the experts said, but sometimes the advice was too confusing or too dogmatic. We listened to all the suggestions from doctors, families, and friends, but soon found that if you ask three people about a problem, you could get four different answers. So we decided to make use of the helpful things we had learned, but also to trust our own instincts and the instincts of our children.

Through our years of parenting, we were very lucky with our children. People complimented us on our skills in parenting. We try to do the best we can. If something works, fine. If not, we try something else. In fact, those were two rules in our home— Rule One: If nothing is wrong with the children, leave them alone. Rule Two: If something is wrong, change the situation.

I decided to outline my parenting philosophy in preparation for my becoming a parenting educator. The basic topics I feel are important form the following chapters of this book. I wanted to give my adult students tangible activities they could do to raise their confidence levels about being parents, so I developed the one hundred and twenty games which offer family members those tangible activities to enhance their parenting skills.

When you have a new baby, you spend most of your time caring for his physical needs. But when your child reaches eighteen months, he is ready to pull away from you. This heretofore totally dependent child asserts himself, and it is not uncommon for you to begin to ask yourself, "Whose child is this?" "How can I have such conflicting emotions of love and annoyance about him?" "What did I do wrong?"

The answers are "yours," "it's normal," and "probably nothing." Your child is just doing what he is supposed to do, and as long as you realize that what you are going through is what most other parents are experiencing, you will feel much better.

Remember when someone warned you that a just-born was wet, bloody, wrinkled, and screaming? You had to change your expectations to realize that before your child is fully grown, he has to pass through stages that may leave you wrinkled and screaming. Or realize his development may leave you humbled at the idea that something at first so helpless can grow into an independent, well-rounded individual.

Of course, there will be good days and bad days and good hours and bad hours. But it is my philosophy that you have it within your power to restructure the situation, changing the bad into the good, the unpleasant into the pleasant. No parent can be perfect, but all parents can be pleasant. And being pleasant is better than the alternatives.

This book consists of practical suggestions you can use to improve and strengthen your family bond. I have used the masculine pronoun when referring to the children merely for grammatical simplification. Boys and girls are equal in this book and in life. I have not included an "ages and stages" chart for two reasons. 1) If your child is already doing what the charts say he should, you know about that stage already. 2) If your child is not yet doing what the chart says he should, your looking at a chart will only make you feel inadequate as a parent or feel that you have a less than wonderful child, neither of which I want you to feel. If you ever feel that your child is not performing at his proper level, consult with an expert in that field. If treatment is necessary, get it. If the experts assure you that nothing is amiss, relax and enjoy your child's own particular development.

So in all the ups and downs of parenting, how can you feel like a winner? You can play these games. They are specific activities to help you through certain situations, to strengthen your good points, and to lessen your weak spots. Since everyone is a winner in these games, the more of them you can play, the easier your family life may be.

When you arm yourself with a combination of a knowledge of parenting skills and a promise to enjoy each stage of your child's development to the fullest, you are well on the road to winning the parenting game.

To determine how you are doing as a parent at this moment, take this "**How Are You Doing**?" test. This is your own parenting 20 questions. The more often you can answer "most of the time" to these questions, the closer you come to being a pleasant parent. Answer each question with a Never (N), Sometimes (S), or Most of the Time (M). Give the test to other members of your family. Discuss the answers. Improve where indicated. Congratulate yourself where indicated.

The "How Are You Doing?" Test

1. Do you remember what it was really like to be a child?
2. Do you admit when you are wrong?
3. Do you avoid sexual stereotypes for toys, occupations, chores, and emotional reaction?
4. Do you get down on the floor to see things from the perspective of your child?
5. Do you stand back before you blow-up?
6. Do you listen for the question behind your child's question?
7. Do you look for the reason behind your child's outburst?
8. Do you occasionally cook what your child does like to eat?
9. Do you give your child choices to make as often as possible?
10. Do you give sympathy when your child needs it?
11. Do you give a hug to your child when he is misbehaving?
12. Do you spend private time with each child?
13. Do you make it easy for your child to talk to you?
14. Do you thank your child for being himself?
15. Do you give your child as much intellectual stimulation as he can accommodate?
16. Do you expose your child to the variety of life?
17. Do you take time for yourself as a person?
18. Do you explain to the family about your roots?
19. Do you avoid terminal seriousness?
20. Do you work on improving your parenting skills?

UPS...AND...DOWNS

Chapter One:
Adjustments

Chapter One:
Adjustments

When you find out that you are pregnant, you celebrate the new life beginning to grow within you. You may have friends and relatives who have children, and they have regaled you with all the good and the bad that being parents entails. But you are determined to be different. Your time as parents will have its ups and downs, but you have decided that you will focus on the ups and try to remember that after every down, there is an up.

Being pregnant and being parents means having to make adjustments: physical, mental, psychological, and financial. In fact, your whole life from this point on will be a series of adjustments.

Both the man and the woman are pregnant, albeit in different senses. Most of the focus is on the mother-to-be, but the father-to-be is certainly as important as he lends his support, shares his emotional changes, and helps to make plans throughout the nine months.

You should both become students of pregnancy, reading the literature about what is happening to your body and your family situation. Both of you should attend prenatal classes, tour the hospital, and become list makers, if you aren't already. Play **"What Questions Should I Ask?"** by making lists of questions to ask the doctor and anyone else with more experience than you have. It is best to get into the habit of writing down both the questions and answers now, because after the baby arrives, your conversations with the doctors and other authorities will be more harried. If you write down the answers and the instructions you are given, you can remember them better.

You will have to make adjustments in your home for the new arrival. Whether the baby will be sharing part of your room or will have a room of his own, you need to make plans about his furniture and his physical space. Those of you who feel superstitious about having anything for the baby in the house before he is born must still do some preparation. Visit the baby goods store, make your selections, and ask that they be delivered after the baby is born. Without this preparatory work now, you will be too exhausted or too busy when you actually are parents. You will be grateful for all of this planning ahead.

As an investment in your physical strength and mental health, you should make arrangements for someone to help out in the home after the mother and baby return from the hospital. Although some people prefer to hire a baby nurse, what you really need is someone to take care of the house and the meals, because you will want to make getting to know your baby your highest priority. The best way to learn is by doing. Whether the husband or one of your mothers or a professional is chosen, you will be relieved that you don't have to worry about all positions on the home front. If you are engaging professional help, you must book early and keep in touch often to make sure about the arrangements. Have backup systems just in case.

You probably will be spending hours looking over lists of names for your child. Play **"How Does This Name Sound?"** Put a name you like next to your last name, and see if it sounds right. Remember that you can never please everyone, no matter what name you choose. There will always be someone who wanted you to name the baby something else. The important thing is for you and your spouse to agree. You may want to follow the suggestion of keeping the choice of a name a secret until the baby has arrived. That way people won't have the luxury of time to express their dissatisfaction. Once the baby is a person with a name, people seem more accepting. However, if anyone gives you any trouble about the name you have chosen, play the **"Good Idea for Next Time"** game. Simply tell them that their favorite name is a good suggestion and that you will keep it in mind when you are planning a name for your next child. You have given no promises, made no insults, but you have maintained your independence and your integrity. This game can be played during any disagreement in the early months of parenthood. "Thank you for your advice. I'll keep it in my mind. I appreciate your expertise." Sometimes you have to do it your way. Sometimes you may want to take advantage of the voice of experience. In any event, you are entitled to make your own mistakes and achieve your own successes.

Another adjustment you both have to make during your joint pregnancy is that of viewing your life together in terms of a third party, the baby. You should have initial talks about parenting philosophies. How might you handle the major subjects of discipline, child care, working outside of the home, religion, relatives, family gatherings, anger? Surely, your opinions on these topics may change as time passes, but it is important to have a sense of direction. When you say before you have a child that you will never allow your child to climb on furniture or that you will never take the baby to the market after dark, you are laying out your expectations. But the school of experience and the internal developmental mechanisms in a child may cause you to change your opinion, sometimes even radically. Never criticize a parent for what he does or doesn't allow his child to do before you have a child. Many times you will have to lower your standards to raise your child. This is because your standards may have been based on ideal situations which rarely apply to child rearing, or they may be formulated before you have a proper knowledge of what a child needs to do as he matures. Be tolerant.

Since pregnancy is a time of emotional turmoil, you may want to organize your thoughts and keep a record of them in a diary. You can explain how you feel, describe the hopes and dreams you have for your child, and discuss your fears. The most frightening times in a pregnancy are at the very beginning, near the end, and when anything goes wrong. Both partners may want to write about, or at the very least discuss, the great deal of attention the woman is receiving and how the man should be remembered during these nine months. Begin to put into action your positive parenting skills with thoughts like these: 1) A pregnant woman's body is never ugly. It is expanding with your child. 2) Mother's milk is the sweetest nourishment imaginable. 3) You are all part of the mystery of life.

Now you are at the tail end of the pregnancy. You have packed your suitcase, practiced all the exercises from the prepared childbirth classes, and all you can do is wait. From this time on, the baby is the boss. When he is ready to be born, he will indicate such. When he is ready to eat or sleep or walk or talk or date, he will let you know. From this point forward, you will be guided by a combination of his cues and your knowledge and experience as parents.

Choose a hospital that allows the husband to be involved. If the husband is not one who feels he can participate, enlist the help of a dear friend. Nowadays, there is no reason to be alone during the birthing process. Both husbands and wives must keep their senses of humor during labor. The more smiles you can summon in the midst of the pain, the happier you will all be. Trust the doctors and attending personnel, but question anything about which you are not sure. You have the right to be informed about all procedures.

The moment of birth is one you will never forget. The immediate bonding of both parents to the newborn is paramount. Look that gorgeous, wrinkled, wet baby in the eyes. Pour all your love and hopes into his heart. Assure him with your wide smile that his world will be wonderful. If you adopt your baby, you will be able to bond with him from the first time you are able to hold him in your arms. That time will be special indeed.

Your stay in the hospital should be one of rest and practice. When the baby doesn't need you, nap, walk, shower, spread the news about your child. If you have had a Caesarean section, follow the doctor's advice. You need the extra time to recuperate. You do not need to prove yourself to anyone, and you should never think of yourself as a failure in delivering. You should focus on the fact that the doctors were able to give you your healthy baby in the safest way for both mother and child.

If there is some medical problem with the baby, inundate the medical staff with your questions, follow through with their suggestions, and find support for yourselves. Many fine groups like Listening Ears or Support Groups for medical problems are available to you. Do not be alone.

When your world calls to discuss the baby, let your amazement at nature permeate your conversations. You have now joined the brotherhood of men or the sisterhood of women stretching back to the beginning of civilization, and neither of you will ever be the same.

As you walk down to the hospital's nursery viewing windows, with each slow step that you take, congratulate yourself for what you have done. Say to each other, "We will make this baby's world wonderful."

It is about at this point that your former sleeping patterns cease to exist. The baby will be brought to you for feedings when the clock registers times you only heard about and never really saw. That nursing or bottling in the wee hours of the night takes some getting used to, but your mandate is to view this as a magic time, a special sharing time when you give life-sustaining force to someone who is totally dependent upon you.

Avail yourself of the training sessions in nursing, feeding techniques, bathing, and use the nurses as important resources. The best training sessions are the ones in which you can practice on your own baby. Carefully observe how the nurses handle the babies. They are decisive and sure and give the babies a great deal of credit for not falling apart.

Sometime during your last night in the hospital, you and your spouse should play **"I'm Proud of You."** You should have a small ceremony in which you tell each other what this birthing experience has meant and how you now feel about each other. You might choose to exchange meaningful gifts, which will carry with them the magic of this moment as you anticipate your parenting years together.

Bringing the baby home entails two rides. The first one is the wheelchair ride out of the hospital. As you carry your baby in your arms, you are really introducing him to the public. You are now "wearing" that bundle on the outside, and you should be beaming with joy. Your next ride is in the car heading for home. The baby should be put in an infant car seat from this moment on. Years later, when he graduates to the seat belt, he will continue his habit of car safety.

He probably will sleep in the car, eat when he arrives home, sleep some more, and not be a problem until he starts screeching in the middle of the night. There must be something about the change in atmosphere from the busy hospital nursery to the quiet of your home, but this heretofore peaceful, placid baby often turns into a terror on his first night home. This phenomenon also has to do with the fact that the baby is probably four days old, and his nervous system is undergoing changes. So how do you cope with your baby at home? You feed him, change him, stroke him, bundle him in a blanket for some extra physical security, give him a pacifier for his additional sucking needs, and relax. There comes many a time when you will have done all you possibly can for the baby and he is still upset. Just go through your procedures like the pro that you now are, and take comfort in the fact that he will eventually calm down.

It is important that when you first arrive at home, some part of the baby equipment is set up. You will need, at the very least, a place for the baby to sleep and a place to change him. Some clothes and some diapers and formula if you are bottling are necessary. It is also a good idea to have a place for him to sleep and to be changed on each level of your house. You will not have the strength to begin preparing a nursery when you arrive at home, nor will you want to climb the stairs many times a day. All three of you will need as much sleep as the baby will allow you to have.

You will want to have visitors and perhaps a religious ceremony to welcome the baby into the world. Enlist the help of others during this time. You do not have to prove yourself to anyone. What you need to do is regain your strength and maintain your glow. The gift acknowledgments and birth announcements and return phone calls are all important, but they can certainly be received a little late.

At first, when your sleep patterns are adjusting to the baby's schedule or lack of one, you will notice that the days and nights merge. There may no longer be a distinction in your mind between day and night, because your existence is now probably divided into four hour shifts. For this reason, it is important that you bathe as often as possible and at the very least change your clothes and the baby's clothes every twelve hours, so it will appear as though a separate night and a separate day have passed.

When the baby is calm and peaceful, you can handle almost anything. But when he is crying, it is a different story. If, after you have tended to all his physical and cuddling needs, he still calls you during the night, you two adults can play **"It's Your Turn Now."** Rotate getting out of bed to see what the problem is. If you can't find anything else wrong, but the baby disagrees, offer him the pacifier, pat him on the back, and return to your room. He'll either stop crying right away, or he won't. The amount of time you let him cry depends on your own nervous system. But you want to avoid the pattern of rocking the baby all night or of carrying him around for hours. He will soon be able to program his internal clock for night sleep, but you all have to have some patience.

The world of infants is divided into two groups, those who sleep through the night and those who do not. We had three children in the latter category and can state that there is no correlation between that group and continued horrendous behavior in later life. They do, however, owe us approximately four years of uninterrupted sleep. If your baby likes to see the stars in the heavens at too-early hours, you have to tend to his needs, unless you choose to ignore him. You can tend to him in one of two ways. The first is the natural way of feeling put-upon and angry that you are being deprived of your sleep. The other is to develop a more pleasant attitude by remembering that this helpless baby really does need you, that you are performing ennobling acts. So instead of having an ax to grind, sharpen your pleasant parenting skills. Find an all-night radio or TV station, fantasize about what the others in the world may be doing right now, tune into the night sounds in your neighborhood, tell the baby your life story, devise a scenario for his future. Pat yourself on the back for having a good attitude during trying times. The baby has to sense your upbeat vibrations and will eventually release you from your middle-of-the-night bondage. Remember that you won't feel so upset after sunrise.

Another problem in the early weeks is colic, a condition of uncomfortable crying which is probably caused by sharp intestinal pains. Babies with colic, which usually only appears during the first three months, are obviously bothered and spread their discomfort throughout the house. You hate to see something so little be in such pain. Some relief may be achieved by taking the baby outside for a walk, placing a ticking clock near his crib, and putting some of mother's perfume on the crib sheets to give a secure reminder that mother is near. The automatic swing (that also has a cradle attachment) often affords peace to the baby because of its soothing rocking motion.

Since the crying of the baby can be so taxing on the parents, you must get out with some regularity. Hire a sitter, or engage a friend who understands that the baby may be crying for several hours. Then go out, and forget about your home obligations until you return.

In fact, the sooner you establish the habit of using a baby-sitter the better. You both are entitled to some part of your life without the baby. And the baby will benefit from getting used to other people around him. He derives stimulation from being around others who cuddle him and relate to him in slightly different ways. You can play **"Pass the Baby"** without feeling any guilt. The baby needs new voices around him, new sights, variations of dark and light colors, different textures, and new smells. His needs for fresh air and stimulation can be met by you or your babysitter. Furthermore, when he is finally sleeping, the noise around him does not seem to bother him one bit. When he is up, he's up, and when he is out, he's out. In fact, you should be careful not to adopt the habit of "hushing" each other or visitors simply because the baby is sleeping. Babies who are used to sleeping through the normal household sounds will retain that ability better than those who live in "quiet" homes.

You will have an on-going relationship with your doctors. You need to feel confident in your dealings with them. You usually take the baby to the pediatrician when he is about a month old. Also take along the list of questions that you have kept over the last weeks. Write down answers and instructions just as you did with the obstetrician. Find out how your doctor handles phone calls. When your baby is sick, you need to describe the symptoms over the phone. He or she is most concerned about pain, fever, and green mucus. Find out whether the doctor doesn't mind giving reassurances over the phone. The best doctors are those who understand the fears and uncertainties of the novice parents and do their best to listen and be helpful.

After you have dealt with the questions you have about your newborn, you may then be able to wonder "How will we parents ever feel like people again?" It is mandatory for you to keep up your physical strength by eating properly and sleeping often. Your emotional well-being is also important. Cry when you feel overwhelmed. Don't keep in the feelings. Discuss your concerns and fears with each other and, if you need to, with someone else who understands. The common post-partum depression, which is caused by your unbalanced hormonal levels after pregnancy, is something you may have to face. I distinctly remember feeling a surge from the bottom of my feet, up through my entire body, and out my eyes in the form of uncontrollable tears. As soon as this happened to me, I realized that it was my post-partum depression, and I began to laugh. My psyche, without my dictating to it consciously, was following what the pregnancy books said would happen. My laughing soon overcame my crying.

If you find it a little harder to shake off the post-partum depression or the feelings of your being an inadequate parent, then the best medicine for you—after you have told your concerned ones how you feel—is to get out of the house. Go for walks with the baby. Show off your treasure. Join an exercise class. Find a playgroup (see chapter on Early Socialization). Do things for yourself. If and when it is your time to work outside of the home, find satisfactory child care. Remember that both parents form a team, the members of which thrive because they lend support to each other when that support is needed.

A major problem that you will experience in the early months of parenting is exhaustion. Keep in mind that torture victims are often deprived of sleep. When you feel exhausted, you are not getting enough deep sleep, and your rapid eye movements or REMs are being interrupted, so your dreaming time is restricted. This lack of REMs contributes to your depressed mood. Your dream deprivation forces you to work through some of your subconscious concerns during the day, so you may feel even more depressed. This depression affects both men and women, but for women, it is even worse, because they have to face another day without much of a break. Furthermore, a woman's hormonal system is currently not in its usual balance because of the pregnancy and delivery. She may feel overwhelmed with depression, sadness, and grief at the memories of how she used to be. One minute she may be crying because everything has gone wrong, the next minute she may be crying with joy that she has such a gorgeous baby. Fortunately, you all can feel much better after some sleep. Nap during the day, even if you have to hire a sitter to do so. Next to eating, sleeping is the most important thing you can do for yourself during these first weeks.

Another way of overcoming exhaustion is to take a fifteen-minute **"Mommy Break"** each morning and each evening. Be alone during this time, and do whatever will make you feel happier (other than sleeping). Take a bubble bath, recline in a candle-lit room, listen to your favorite music, read. Do whatever it takes to make you feel more like a human again. You need to regain some sense of self after the experience of being a new mother. If the father is the primary caregiver in the early weeks, then he should take a **"Daddy Break"** twice a day.

A further problem you may find is that you no longer have a sex life. One of you is, or maybe both of you are, probably so exhausted from the birth and the emotional demands of your infant that making love may be the farthest thing from your mind. Or it may be the farthest thing in only one of your minds and the closest thing in your partner's mind. So you must be honest with your partner. "I'm just too tired." "The thought of doing something for one more person today makes me sick." "I feel my body is too ugly for you to love any more." "I feel you spend too much time with the needs of the baby and not enough with my needs." "I'm afraid the baby will hear us or that we won't hear the baby." No, you are not the only ones who have had these thoughts. Yes, the passage of time will mend some of these problems. But, for now, hire a sitter for the evening. This evening. Or go out tonight for only one hour if you simply can't be away for longer. Go to a place where you can sit facing each other. Play **"Parents Without Children."** Hold hands. Pretend you don't have children for a minute. About what would you talk? What national, world, or personal topics would you have discussed before you had children? Talk about those issues now. Then stare into each other's eyes for a minute. Tell each other three things you love about him or her. Say three things you miss doing with him or her.

Then do something silly on the spur of the moment such as taking the elevator to the top floor of the tallest building in town. Skip across the street. Eat dessert in one restaurant, and then go to another one for a second dessert. Ask people leaving a theater what they thought about the movie. In other words, do something fun that has nothing to do with having had a baby. When you realize that you can still have fun as a well-rounded person, you will begin to feel more like your old self again.

If a kiss in the doorway is all you can muster for now, all right. Since you were honest with your partner, he or she will understand. If your night out leads you to further physical intimacy, that's all right, too. Also, for nights spent at home, remember the allures of candlelight and your favorite music. You don't have to forget that you are parents, but you certainly deserve a break from the pressures and tensions that come with this full-time job.

So now you realize that making adjustments is part of what parenting means. Your entire life has changed, but it certainly is worth all the trouble. The bundle you hold in your arms says it all as he stares up at you. From the moment of your positive pregnancy test, you must set yourselves on the positive course of parenting. Find the pleasantness in all you do together, in the miracle of life, and even in the smallest daily achievement.

WORLD EXPLORER

Chapter Two: Early Socialization

Chapter Two:
Early Socialization

Every parent hopes that his baby will grow up to be happy. We bond to him. We try to meet his every physical need, and we give him emotional nourishment as well. When he is a helpless infant, it seems easier to attend to him, especially when he repays us with his wide smile. However, our job becomes harder when he reaches the negative stage around age two.

The terrible twos, which can begin at eighteen months and last until two-and-a-half or six depending on your perspective, are hard for everyone. But, if you understand that your toddler must go through this stage in his development to become a more independent person, you will be able to live through his demands more easily. How can you turn the terrible twos into a more pleasant time? You can by remembering that your child is doing his baby work. His job is to grow. You can measure his physical changes in inches and pounds. But his emotional growth can only be seen in how he reacts to situations.

It is his job to play **"World Explorer."** That is why your cupboards are untidy, your newspapers are either ripped or on a high shelf, and your sense of any previous housekeeping order is mightily diminished. He must feel, taste, and poke everything. And he must grow away from total dependency on you.

When you hear his "No" to everything, take a step back from the situation. Put your ego on hold. You are not the one who needs to grow up right now. Let him have his "Nos," and be proud that he has the inner drive to mature. Change your tactics when he is being defiant. Don't ask him questions that will need a "yes" or a "no" answer. Give him a choice. "Do you want the toast or the muffin?" "Should we read your book before or after you are in your pajamas?" "Do you want to go to the market now or in five minutes?" By using these semantic tricks, you can often avoid getting into power struggles.

But struggles and tantrums are inevitable. If you feel his tantrum is for attention or for manipulation of you or the circumstances, your best bet is to ignore his crying and screaming. Take him or yourself to another room until one of you feels human enough to carry on. If the tantrum is the result of the child's feelings of frustration or inadequacy, then you may want to administer hugs and sympathy. It is very important to reassure any terrible-two-year-old even though he has been horrendous that you still love him, no matter what and forever. "You had a hard day today. I feel sad when you have a tantrum, but I know you are growing up. Maybe tomorrow will be a better day. I love you."

Your child's explorations and frustrations and achievements are all normal parts of his maturing. He is becoming a social person, and your job is to provide him with the necessary socialization through activities and experiences.

In earlier times, when man lived in tribes, or even later when the family unit was extended, a child's socialization practically took place by itself. But today's society is different. We have to make more of a formal effort to facilitate the socialization of our children.

One of the best ways to foster socialization is to become part of a playgroup. A playgroup is simply a gathering of similar age children and their primary caregivers, usually the mothers. Both of you need a playgroup. It offers the baby his initiation into the fellowship of his colleagues. It offers the parents a number of friends who can provide support. You will realize that you are not the only ones who are going through a particular stage. You will realize that you are good parents and that your child can function outside of your home.

Especially in the lonely first years of first parenting, you need a support group. Whether you start or join a group that is informal or formal, it doesn't matter. The fact that you are out and with others who are parents is what is important. Those mothers who work also out of the house do have the psychological lift of having their sanity validated by the outside world. But those same mothers also need to commune with parents to keep their domestic sanity.

For those of you who, for whatever reason, find it impossible to join a playgroup, you need to go out of the house and be with others. Some good places to meet your colleagues are the library, especially at story time, the park, the mall, the community center, toddler gym classes, other baby classes, and the pet store. Play **"Pick Up a Date"** for you and your child by exchanging phone numbers (just when you thought you were done with the dating game!). The point is to meet friends for yourself and your baby. Many a lifelong friendship has started this way, not to mention some marriages.

But the best thing is to become part of a playgroup. Each one is a bit different. Some mothers want to remain with the group the whole time. Others relish the idea of the ones in which they can leave for "free time" when they are not one of the designated mothers on duty. Some groups schedule a topic for discussion while others enjoy unstructured conversations.

Find an appropriate group. Loneliness for new parents is harmful to everyone's mental health. As soon as you feel you are ready to join a playgroup (and as soon as you are home alone with your infant isn't too early), find one or start your own. Advertise in local papers, or find someone in the neighborhood who seems to have his or her finger on the pulse of the babyhood situation. Reach out for contacts. You will be so glad you did. The same is true for joining babysitting co-ops. For some people, these group-sharing times for babysitting afford them the opportunity of going out without the problems of having inexperienced sitters.

When you are in a playgroup, you should spend your time enjoying the group situation. Your child will be practicing socialization at various developmental levels. A baby first engages in solitary play by himself even if he is in a group. He is being social, but he is on his own. As he gets a little older, he will have parallel play. That is, he and his friends may be working on puzzles or playing with trucks separately while they sit together. Color and sound sensations are important at this stage. Later, they move to associative play where there is some interaction based on skill levels. The final stage is the more formal cooperative play where they exchange ideas as they pretend. This range of types of play covers the pre-school years. So, depending on what age your child enters a group setting, you will know what type of play you should expect to observe.

One of the least pleasant aspects of the group experience for everyone concerned is the problem of sharing. Adults want children to be able to share, because the little ones need to know how to live in a society of give and take, not just take and take. The babies and toddlers, on the other hand, are just at the stage of "I" development. They are working out what belongs to them, what is part of them, and what is an extension of them. Before they have solved some of the problems of life, they still think that their toys are part of them. So, from their point of view, why should they have to let someone else play with part of them? When they reach the level of knowing where they end and the toys begin, they are actively engaged in working out what exactly is their territory. Their friends may be threats to them during this period. Only when you can reason with them and when they no longer feel threatened can sharing blossom. In the meantime, parents still need to pull out the abhorrent weeds of grabbing and hoarding. Once you have an understanding of why they don't share automatically, you can feel better about their group experiences.

When he reaches that point of understanding about sharing, he still may need some reminders about social graces. Play **"All But One"** by explaining "When your friends come over today, they may play with all of your toys except the special one we put on your bed." This way he is able to make some decision about which toy is too important for him to allow another human being to touch. Teddy bears often fall into this category, as do a few special birthday gifts. After all, you don't allow your guests to touch everything in your home when they come to visit.

Other social graces are necessary during the playgroup. If your child isn't saying "thank you" and "please" and "bye-bye" on his own, at least if you remind him at the proper times to say these words, the other adults present will know that you are trying to instill manners.

The parents of the group should decide at the beginning what forms of discipline should be used, especially if some of the parents leave during the group time. Of course, you will all use positive reinforcement, separation from the scene of the crime, and hugs rather than hits. Never belittle the child who is grabbing or hitting, because sooner or later, your child will do those same things. Have compassion for what the parent of the grabber must be feeling. Remember that it is normal for children to go through such stages of behavior. But they must be taught over and over the more acceptable forms of social interaction. The day will dawn when they actually do hand a toy to a friend and say, "Would you like to play with this toy?"

To prevent major outbursts of anger and grief when activities are being changed or even when it is time to leave, you can play **"Two Minute Warning."** Tell your child that he has two more minutes to play before it will be snack time, or remind him that he will be going home in two more minutes. Then one minute, then time is up. The more he can know what is going to happen and when, the better for everyone.

Your job as parent in the playgroup is to be supportive of what the other mothers are doing, to give suggestions in pleasant ways when you feel something needs to be changed, and to be proud of your child. Don't be overprotective. Let him try going down the slide backwards if he wants to. This is his laboratory. He is a scientist in search of his limits. Enjoy observing him and his peers, because before you know it, he will be too old for this type of situation.

Another wonderful avenue for socialization is the parent-child class. When my children were each two years old, I was fortunate to attend the Parent-Child Development classes run by the adult education department of Montgomery County Public Schools (Maryland). In these classes, which were set up like nursery school rooms, we played together in structured and unstructured activities, and then the parents met for discussions of pertinent topics.

The advantage of taking any parenting class is that you realize that you are having the same problems as other parents. You are not alone in a parenting group. The advantage of bringing the children to the parenting class is that your skilled teacher can watch your interaction and give you praise when you so desperately need it during the early, lonely years of parenting. Your child has the advantage of socialization, and so do you. Even if you work full time, you still need something like a parenting class to allow you to touch base with the issues with which you must deal.

When I was asked to teach parenting, I wrote a statement of philosophy and a class schedule which was based on similar classes. They are reprinted here to reinforce the advantages a parenting group supplies.

PHILOSOPHY OF THE PARENT-CHILD NURSERY

What excitement! You and your baby have reached quite a milestone. He is ready for group socialization. You realize that he is really growing up.

You may be asking, "What do we do now?" You've read all the "ages and stages" books, but all of a sudden, you are finding that your baby is becoming more complicated. How can something so little and so cute evoke in you such conflicting emotions of love and annoyance? This baby is becoming a child.

Raising a child is the most important, rewarding, and frustrating job we will encounter. Yet it is the one for which we are least trained. Even after we read all the literature, which is at times contradictory, we still are faced with unanswered questions and gnawing doubts, which are always coupled with unlimited love.

It is the purpose of this class to allow you to express in a supportive environment concerns about parenting and to search for possible answers, to realize that others are experiencing your same problems and emotions, to observe your child in age appropriate activities in a group setting, to form friendships, and to revel in the joy of your child.

Based on what you give and receive in a setting of support and informed communication, it is hoped that you will improve your sense of parenting and strengthen your family bond.

CLASS PROCEDURES OF PARENT-CHILD NURSERY

Welcome to your parenting class! We, as parents, are at the same time both experts and novices. So we come together as students in our adventure. Here are the class procedures.

1. Home Preparation- Do talk about class to your child often during the week. He will develop a sense of class as a special "big boy" time you share together.
2. Themes- Each class will revolve around a theme like hands, squares, autumn leaves, holidays.
3. Activity Time- The first part of the class will be parent-child activities. Small muscle control, sensory awareness, rhythm, movement, and socialization will be developed through related activities and toys. Instructional hints will be written near the projects, so parents will be able to guide the children. If he does not want to participate in an activity, it is all right. Eventually, he may follow your example of participating.
4. Clean-Up- Parents help in the cleaning up. Some day, children may realize that this is a necessary part of life.

5. Circle Time- This togetherness time is when we will build self-esteem, sing, and hug.
6. Snack- A small snack and drink will be served.
7. Discussion Time During Free Play- The child will engage in large muscle play while parents have discussions on parenting. If a child wants to sit on your lap and screech the whole time, that is all right with me. I will keep the discussions going through any volume of noise. At times, the room might even be quiet! Don't worry if your child is having a "bad day." We all have them, so we understand.
8. Clean-Up II
9. Goodbye Time- We will say goodbye with circle games, songs, and hugs.
10. Home Reinforcement- Children love to hear the class songs between sessions. Daddies and grandparents should share in the excitement of the child's new learning experiences.
11. Give and Take- Parents should be willing to share strengths and weaknesses, be willing to make friends, be willing to enjoy yourselves and your children. Communication is paramount.

Whichever you choose to join or start—your own playgroups, babysitting co-ops, or parenting classes—you will be giving yourself and your child the gift of socialization. Neither of you will be lonely. You will be able to take pride in watching the children romp together like a pride of young lion cubs. Moreover, you should feel an emotional high from your socialization with other parents. You should come away from your group situation feeling three things– that your child is like everyone else, that your child is special, and that you are blessed to have such a child.

THE DAILY ROUTINE

Chapter Three:
Routines

Chapter Three:
Routines

When I taught high school at the beginning of my career, the emphasis was on objectives. They had to be stated clearly so that the student knew what was expected of him. I carried over this technique when I became a parent. Everyone likes to know what is going to happen, and when you are in charge of a family, you need to communicate plans and procedures to your group. If you have those objectives clearly in your own mind, your life will be easier.

When you first become a parent, you quickly learn what a baby's schedule entails. The feeding, the changing, the dressing, the bathing all need to be done at certain times. I can remember feeling so overwhelmed at the constant care a baby needs that I thought I would never get the dinner table set. After the first few weeks passed, I had lowered my expectations and felt a strong sense of accomplishment if I could take care of the laundry before the end of the day.

Then a wonderful thing happened. The baby became a little less demanding. I actually saw that my day could be divided into time periods. I found that if I viewed the day in several sections, the idea of being alone with a baby did not seem so overwhelming. The daily organizational ideas which follow were very helpful to me and my family.

Our wake-up activities included hugs, diaper changing, getting dressed, breakfast, music, tidying up, television, and whatever house chores needed to be done. Then we were ready for our morning outing. Whether you use this time to meet your needs or those of your child or even a combination of the two, you should look forward to this time.

On the morning outing, if your two-year-old complains about having to go to one more store, give him an enjoyable job. Play the game where he is the **"Green Detective"** who has to look for all the things that are green in the store. Or have him make the decisions like which door should you open, which aisle should you go down next, which elevator you should use. Remember that he probably could use some channeling of ideas and that he certainly gets tired before you do.

After the morning outing, we would come home for lunch-and-a-nap. Those four words always went together in our home. When your child no longer takes a nap, you can introduce "rest time," the concept that the child goes to his room and does something that is befitting quiet time: playing with toys, looking at the pictures in books, taking out all the clothes in his drawers, or even crying, if he feels that is necessary. You are entitled to your rest time away from him. Whenever you two decide that the nap or rest is over, you should have had enough of a break to return to him feeling refreshed and eager to face the next part of the day.

During the afternoon activity, whether it be a trip to the back yard, a visit with some playmates, a carpool drive to pick up siblings, or a nature walk up the street, you can point out the wonders of the world. Ask your toddler why the traffic lights swing back and forth. Bend down to his level, and see what he sees. Collect treasures on a nature walk. Listen to the birds overhead or the trucks on the highway. Talk about the shapes of the clouds. Smell the evergreen trees. Feel the blades of grass or the icicles near the window. Inundate his senses. Ask him his opinion of things. Fill his brain.

Quiet time can be next: story telling, book reading, music listening, television watching, hugging. Arts and crafts, depending on the age of your child, can consist of simple crayon marks on plain paper or pasting down the leaves you collected on your nature walk. You can draw an elaborate maze for him to follow or color in. You can cut out three shapes for him and have him manipulate them on a paper to form interesting scenes. Homemade play dough has a wonderful texture and can be reused often. Just make it a different color from the floor above which it will be used. Here is an easy recipe. Stir over low heat, and knead the following– 3 cups flour, 1 and 1/2 cups salt, 6 teaspoons cream of tartar, 3 cups water mixed with at least 40 drops food coloring, and 3 tablespoons cooking oil.

Continuing with the day's activities, I usually made dinner while the children were watching "Sesame Street." But I quickly learned that when they wanted my attention during meal preparation, they wouldn't stop until they had my attention. This period of late afternoon tiredness, low blood sugar level, and tension because they shouldn't eat another snack so close to dinner forms the murky basis for what has been labeled the Arsenic Hour. Ours usually was from 5:00 to 6:00. Sometimes it was from 4:00 to 7:00. But it hit us with regularity. When I was too tired to care, I would just let everyone get on each other's nerves, knowing that when Daddy came home and we ate dinner, all would be forgotten. But when I was feeling on top of the situation, I would engage the children in kitchen helper projects. Our bottom cabinet was our toddler's office. He would take out all the plastic containers, stack them for castles, bat them down with a rolling pin, or make mazes out of the silverware. Bowls became helmets or pretend bathtubs.

Another idea for this time of day is water play. Be sure to turn the kitchen chair around so that the back is up against the counter. So what if he gets wet? At least he has been occupied for several minutes. The value of water play cannot be underestimated. Watch a child's face as he stares at the dripping or running water. His fascination with science will carry over to feeling the temperature, splashing, making waves, filling up cups, spilling out. Be sure to warn him about the danger of hot water. His unmitigated pleasure is worth the little bit of time it takes you to wipe up half of your house.

On warm days, let him paint the sidewalk with water on large paint brushes or draw with chalk.

Another good project for him to do while you are in the kitchen is playing with unpopped corn or uncooked rice. Spread an old tablecloth out on the floor. Pour the corn or the rice into a bowl. Add measuring cups, spoons, containers, sieves, and anything else you want. Yes, the contents will spill, but it only takes a few minutes of cleaning up. In the meantime, he has been busy doing his "work" for a long while.

If you have the patience to allow him to "help" you with the actual cooking, you will be amazed at the fun you two can have together. You can do the dangerous things like cutting and going near the stove, but he can stir, peel, mix, shake, and decide which spice you should add to the recipe. You can also give an interesting science lesson about changes in texture as well as a mathematics demonstration about measuring. When you decide that your child can be a helper rather than an annoyance in the kitchen, then your Arsenic Hour will be greatly diminished.

When Daddy arrived home, I always breathed a sigh of relief and congratulated myself for making it through another day. It is at this point that you no longer have the full responsibility for caring for your child. The **"Greeting Daddy"** ceremony should be at the very minimum a hug and a kiss between the two parents, followed by one for each of the children. We like sandwich kisses where we rotate who is the bread and who is the filling. In any event, everyone should have a turn. Of course, you know that each family member is loved, but you have to provide a tangible proof like this greeting does each day. Depending on when the meal is ready, you could expand the ceremony to include a run-down of the day's activities or you could wait for a telling of your day's events during the meal.

No matter how easy or hard a day the husband has had, he must remember that part of his fathering job is to be an active father the minute he steps in the door. The mother must remember that no matter how hard a day she has had, she should wait awhile before reciting the chronology of horrors she has witnessed that day.

Dinner should be a time when each family member has a chance to share ideas. The problem is that in the early years, the baby is having his fussy time during the meal or the toddler is going through his "I wouldn't consider eating anything green" stage. Maybe you'll be lucky enough to be on diets, so that you can finish the meal quickly!

The routine after dinner should give everyone a secure feeling. I used to love to do the dishes, because that meant that my husband was with the children and I didn't have to be. That is a common feeling if you have been with them all day. If you are a single parent or one who does not have such relief in the evenings, you need to find some way to relax either with or without the children around.

Daddy and the children would play in the back yard and do the gardening in the warm weather. When it was time to be indoors, they would have roughhousing on the floor, engage in games of **"Try to Take Off Daddy's Sock,"** read stories, and play board games. I would join in when my chores were done and I felt a bit rejuvenated.

When the children were pre-schoolers, we liked to wind down their days by having a circle time singing their favorite songs.

The rituals of bathtime and bedtime vary with each family. When the children are in the bath, you should take a moment each time to stare at their beautiful bodies and admire the handiwork of nature. The hugs and kisses at bedtime make your child feel secure. Whether you couple them with reading a story or singing a song, your children should realize how much they are loved. We would always tell them one activity that was scheduled for the next day. The last thing we would see on their faces was a smile of anticipation as they closed their eyes.

That scene seems idyllic. But what about the child who cries at bedtime? The way I see it, you have two possible courses of action. You can be soft, or you can be firm. As terrible as it sounds, I recommend that you be firm.

What that means is you first try to find out why the child is crying. If he is an infant or baby, of course you check for hunger, wetness, or danger in the crib. Then you should kiss him in the crib and leave the room. Whether you put some of the mother's perfume on the sheets, so it seems as though part of her is around, or you leave on a night light, you have done all you should. So leave his room. Those parents who try to rock the baby to sleep and then put him down in the crib only to cringe as he starts to cry again slowly come to the same conclusion. You have done all you can for the baby, so he has to calm down himself. Even if he cries for twenty minutes (and you won't be able to stand it after the first ten), he will eventually stop. He needs to become self-sufficient unless you want to pretend to go to sleep with him for the next several months.

As he matures and develops fears, he may need you to reassure him. His fears are real to him. So you can open the closet door to let out the monsters. You can keep on the light the whole night. You can hang up a bad-guy-keeper-awayer near his window. But you must remain firm. He cannot sleep in your bed, and he cannot keep coming out of his room.

You will thank yourselves for being firm at bedtime. When they are all asleep, you finally have time for yourselves and for each other. But do you have any strength? I always rejuvenated myself for a few hours by reading, writing, watching television, or doing crafts. During this quiet time, my husband and I would be able to catch up on world events, family matters, and each other.

The routines described in this chapter afford the child a varied set of activities, give you blocks of time to fill rather than having you be overwhelmed by the thought that you have to care for a child forever, and provide outlets that should stimulate all the members of the family. Of course, flexibility and spontaneity should be injected often. But if your children know what is expected of them and what will happen to them, their lives will be more meaningful, and you will feel better about your role as parents.

READY!

Chapter Four: Toilet Training

Chapter Four:
Toilet Training

It is not usual for a bride or a groom to walk down the aisle in diapers. Children usually don't even go to kindergarten in diapers. So why then will your child be the first?

If you are in the midst of trying to toilet train your child, you are probably thinking these same thoughts. Your child will be toilet trained. The only question is when. The only answer is *when he is ready*.

How can someone so small make such a decision? It is his body, his muscles, and his waste products. This activity represents one of the first times he can assert himself over his body and, if you let him, over you.

It is your job to educate him about toilet etiquette and procedures and then give as much positive reinforcement as is humanly possible. Many fine books both for you and your child explain the different methods of toilet training. Your job is to find the best approach for you. I like the following methods.

The world is divided into two camps— those whose children were trained quickly and those whose children were not. My favorite story is about the daddy who said to his two-year-old, "Honey, here are some big-girl underpants. I want you to start wearing them and using the toilet from now on." She did. That scene happened in my cousin's house, not in mine.

I used to think that if only we were living in the times of the cave men who didn't use toilets, my child wouldn't stand out by looking so tall in his diapers. Then when he finally was trained, I felt truly liberated.

At what age do you begin to toilet train? You surely have heard stories about how this one was trained by nine months and that one by the first birthday. If these stories are true, they certainly represent the rare exception, not the rule.

You should start the learning process at the point when you and your child are ready. When your child can point to his diaper to show discomfort, he is probably aware that there is something in it. Sometimes, a slightly older child will be repulsed by brown food or clothing, because he is equating it with bowel movements. Some children show readiness signs by wanting to copy what you do on the toilet. When some signs appear, gear up your patience, and buy a potty seat.

There are two kinds. The one that rests on top of the toilet itself has the advantage of letting the child use the same facility as adults or older siblings. However, some children prefer to have their feet touch the floor for better balance. The freestanding potty seat is more their size. I bought both and gave my children the choice of which one they wanted to use each time. When you first introduce the seat, let your inquisitive child play **"Seat Exploration."** Let him play with it in any way he wants. Let him become familiar with the feel, the parts, the shape.

Then explain to him that you will spend special time with him in the bathroom. Bring in his favorite books or toys. Take off his diaper, and put him on the potty seat. Let him sit there while you read or play the game. Let him explore the world of toilet paper. Stay as long as his attention span will allow. Hug and kiss him for trying. Repeat the process later in the day. If he has a bowel movement at a regular time, try to anticipate his schedule.

After what may seem like years of repeating this futile process, one day something will appear in the potty seat or toilet. Certainly this happening is cause for much praise and reinforcement. But your child is not trained yet. This is just a drop in the bucket compared to what is to come. Your goal is to get him to tell you when he has to go to the bathroom. And only he knows.

Sometimes he doesn't care at all about going. Sometimes he is too busy to remember. Sometimes he doesn't realize how long the car trip will be. For these reasons, I feel that you need to establish **"Trying Times"** when, although he may not think he has to go, he at least has to try. Even if nothing comes out, praise him for trying.

If you have started the process and have had nothing but frustration and tears from either or both of you, then stop. Play **"Start Again in a Few Weeks."** You are in competition with the terrible twos, which will diminish in intensity at some point. When you do restart, pretend it is the first time, and be as cheerful and as easygoing as possible. Your emotional scars heal more easily than his. His need to have a good feeling about himself is more important than your need to have him out of diapers.

He may bring his vivid imagination with him into the bathroom. Will he be flushed away? What goes in the toilet was his possession, so if it is flushed away, will all of his things be flushed away also? Some reassurance that he is such a big boy that he can't go down the hole or that his waste products and toilet paper and water are the only things that are allowed in a toilet may be necessary.

The next big decision is yours. When do you put him in training pants or regular underpants? When he has had several dry diapers is a good time to try. Speak in non-judgmental statements: "Diapers are for when you are not toilet trained. Underpants are for when you use the toilet." Try not to go back to using diapers during the day after you have switched to pants.

Night is a different story. If his diapers are soaking wet in the morning, he probably is not ready to go without diapers at night. Try limiting his liquid intake close to bedtime. Maybe wake him up to use the toilet before you go to bed. If nothing seems to work, have patience, and keep a plastic sheet under the regular sheets. Also, when accidents do happen, and they are bound to, treat them matter-of-factly. He'll be upset enough already without having to hear a lecture from you. If bed-wetting persists for what you think is much too long a time, consult your pediatrician.

Whether you follow the ideas given in the literature about trying to train in one day or employ the concept of taking cues from the child, you will be relieved when the whole business is finally finished. In the meantime, you will, out of necessity, learn the location of the bathrooms in every mall and restaurant in your general neighborhood.

Sometimes, the training is going very well until some cataclysmic occurrence like the birth of a sibling. Don't be surprised if there is regression during times of stress. Some experts say that the birth of a sibling may have just the opposite effect on your child. He may want to prove that he is no longer a "baby" who needs to wear diapers anymore. That certainly wasn't the case in my house. My daughter thought it was cute to compare the size of the newborn diapers with the size of hers. Our closet looked like a warehouse for a diaper company until she ultimately saw the light.

The day I did finally send her to nursery school in big-girl underpants, I worried the whole time that she would come home with wet pants. But that day there was a surprise thunderstorm as she was getting into the carpool driver's car to be driven home. When she opened our front door, she was soaking wet all over except for her underpants!

The basic rule to remember is to be patient. If the training is taking place over several weeks or even over several months, you and your child are bound to feel frustrations. However, it can be harmful if you resort to punishment or threat. He just may not be ready to assert full control over his bathroom needs. If you add the worry that he might not be able to go to nursery school or day camp unless he is trained, you run the risk of overloading his psyche. Then his self-esteem can only suffer. Try some motivational techniques like a bathroom chart. Let him put a star or a sticker up each time he uses the toilet. Give him a bonus on the chart if he goes on his own.

When you accentuate the positive, remain pleasant, and give him credit for his own feelings, you will both have a better time in this department. By the way, I have never heard a child answer "yes" when asked, "Do you have to go to the bathroom?" You will get extra parenting points if you can think of creative ways to get him to that necessary room. Months after he is trained, the day will come when you will look back and ask yourself, "What was all the fuss about?"

CIRCLE TIME

Chapter Five: Nursery School

Chapter Five:
Nursery School

There is no law that says you have to send your child to nursery school. You have been his teacher since he was born. You can continue to be his only one until he reaches the mandatory age for school, or you can send him to nursery school.

The often heard complaints about nursery school are:

1) I can do a better job than the teacher can.
2) He is too young to go.
3) He doesn't need it yet.
4) He'll learn bad things from the other students.
5) I'll miss him.

All these statements may be true, but your child can benefit from the socialization that a school setting can provide. If he is not in a playgroup or similar situation, then he needs nursery school. Besides, nursery school is fun, and it is for only a few hours a day.

How do you know which school is right for you and your child? The first rule is to choose one that is close to where you live or work. If it is not convenient to get to the school, you are placing too much of a burden on yourself. Keep in mind your other obligations, carpools, current siblings, and future infants.

Now that you have narrowed down your choices, you are ready to visit the schools. Always call the director to set up an appointment. Make a list of the questions you would like answered. Some typical concerns are:

1) What can you offer my child? You want to hear things like a warm, supportive, loving environment, socialization, and large and small muscle projects.

2) What are the class activities? You want to hear things like circle time, sharing, calendar work, drawing, gluing, painting, pretending, building, imagining, and listening.

3) What is the child-adult ratio? Whatever you are comfortable with is fine. Most places need to meet state requirements in this area.

4) How are problems handled? Is there a time-out corner? Is discipline handled in a positive manner? Are there "O.K. mistakes"? How is the parent notified?

5) What is emphasized in the school's philosophy? Is it primarily religious or educational or Montessori or hang-loose or a combination?

6) What is the registration procedure? So what if you have to get in line at 6:30 in the morning? It is just one morning of your life.

Your next step is to observe the classrooms. They should meet community standards. They should have sunlight, color, and cheer. Children's pictures should be on display. There should be toys for imagination and manipulation. There should be a quiet corner for storybooks and a noisy corner for pretending. The children should be interacting with each other. The teacher should be involved, but not hovering.

Be at the school during drop-off or pick-up time. Play **"Fill Me In"** by asking several parents to tell you two good things about this school and two bad things about it. Listen to the gossip in the doorways. But keep in mind that everyone has an off-day. Take everything you hear with a grain of salt. Don't sign up because of one wonderful teacher. Suppose she is not there next year? Sign up because you feel they will love your child there and you will feel comfortable leaving him there.

When the time comes for the first day of school, your child will either be brave as can be or as afraid as can be. It seems as if there is no middle ground. Part of the reaction is because of your child's present fears. Part of the reaction is because of your preparation of him.

He can easily sense anxiety in you. Be matter-of-fact. Show him the room ahead of time. Explain what activities he might do. Say things like "Will you draw a picture for me in class?" or "When I come back after class, will you tell me what color shirt your teacher wore?" Tell him where you will be while he is at school. Tell him when you will come back for him. "Mommy always comes back" is quite reassuring. Tell him you will miss him very much while he is at school.

If he is completely hysterical at the class door, follow the teacher's lead. She may ask you to stay for a while, but many experts frown on this technique. She may take your screeching bundle from you and close the door. It is her job to calm him down. That is why she is the teacher. Don't be embarrassed by the crying. Everyone has heard it before, and sooner or later the upset child will join in the activities. Actually, you can feel proud that your child realizes how wonderful your home environment is and how much he would rather be there right now!

If you understand that it is normal for children to feel uncomfortable at the separation, you can better understand why they behave as they do. You might suggest that they take a special toy or stuffed animal along in the car with them to ease the transition. You can reassure them of your return by giving them something from your purse or pocket that they will have to return to you at the end of the class.

Your rapport with the teacher centers around the door. She should kneel down to your child's eye level to greet him. You should have a kind word each day for her. A daily "thank you" can go a long way. It is within your rights to ask a quick "how's he doing?" However, it is within her rights to give a brief answer until it is conference time.

When you do have a problem or concern, go to her directly as your first step. Use confronting skills that allow her to retain her dignity and do not make you embarrass yourself. As the expression goes: You get more with honey than with vinegar. Of course, you can be upset, because she is dealing with your most precious thing, your child, but remember that she is a human being and may even be a parent. I have heard of many nasty parent-teacher meetings, and I know that only hard feelings can be built on a basis of attack and anger. So express your concerns, but try to do so in a non-judgmental way with an emphasis on being able to work out the problem.

You have the right to expect from the teacher a knowledge of your child's actions and reactions. If she communicates regularly with the parents, she can avoid many misunderstandings. Perhaps she can list the month's activities in a letter home, or she can put a sign on the class door telling of that day's projects. You can feel comfortable if the day's adventures alternate between small motor and large motor activities, quiet and noisy tasks, structure and free-play, with story time, snacks, and fresh air included.

You must remember that just as children walk and talk at slightly different times, so do they develop in their social and intellectual timetables. Don't expect more from your child than he is able to give. Enjoy the level at which he performs. He will change, and you will miss the things he used to do.

During the scheduled parent-teacher conference listen, take notes, ask questions. Don't be offended if she offers some room for growth or suggests some further testing. She is a professional and is on your side. You share an ultimate goal– that your child have a positive experience in class.

In fact, part of your assignment should be to try to turn any negative happening into a positive experience. For example, perhaps there is a child in the class who pushes down the blocks when others are trying to build with them. Over the course of several days, your child comes home upset about this problem. Instead of making derogatory statements about that other child who is really crying out for attention, suggest that your child play **"Include the Outsider"** in the block corner. Maybe the negative behavior will stop. Maybe it won't. But at least you have tried to steer the problem into a positive experience rather than reinforcing the negative.

If your child is the block pusher or the bully of the week, you need to suggest some positive ways for him to become involved in the class. Try a chart where he can put a star or a sticker up each day he can report to you something he did that was positive. Working with the teacher can only make all of you feel better. Progress will come.

Your support at home is important. All children go through the stage of not wanting to go to school and of "hating" everything. In fact, your child will go through this stage four or seven or fifteen times in his school career. Each time, there may be something really bothering him. So this is where you use your active listening skills to get at the source of the problem. In any event, you must remain pleasantly adamant that it is his responsibility to go to school and that he must meet his responsibility.

When you ask children what they did in school, you get one of two kinds of answers. They may speak for twenty minutes non-stop, describing every detail of the day, at which point you are sorry you ever asked. Or they may say "nothing." If they say "nothing," it is not because they didn't do anything. It is because you are asking the question wrong. Avoid asking questions requiring a "yes" or "no" answer.

Rephrase your question. "What did you draw with the crayons today?" "Who was the calendar girl?" "What was your snack?" "Who was absent?" "What did you do after you put away the blocks?" You should be familiar enough with the daily procedure to be able to ask these kinds of questions. They should elicit more than one-syllable answers.

Sometimes your child will be too tired to talk about school directly after it ends. Respect his feelings, and ask him when he has re-gathered his resources.

Nursery school is a place of joy, sand, dirt, spilled paint, sharing, and growth. Let your child be a complete student there. Don't stifle him. For example, if your child comes home with sand in his shoes, don't scold him for getting the sand all over the rug at home. It was his job to get the sand in his shoes. Simply empty them before you even go into the house, thereby allowing him to do his child-work and allowing you to keep your rugs intact.

Make a fuss over his projects. Hang some in your home in an art corner. Yes, it is all right to throw away 99% of the work. Otherwise, you'll have no place to walk in a few years. Maybe, each weekend the whole family can gather to look at the art gallery, and then your budding artist can play **"Keep Any Two."** He will be allowed to choose two pictures or projects he wants to keep. The rest may then be discarded.

So your job as the parent of a nursery schooler is to give support to your child, feedback to his teacher, and compliments to yourself that your child is big enough and mature enough to walk down the corridor with the rest of his class. The poignant thing to remember is that before you know it, he will be too old to be in that hallway at all.

SPILLS

Chapter Six:
Discipline

Chapter Six:
Discipline

Nobody said that being a parent would be fun and games all the time. Because children are children and will misbehave, you need to discipline them. Next to hating mucus and dust, I hate having to discipline. I behave, so why can't my children? Well, the facts are that I am not faultless and neither are my children. Growing up is about finding your way on the path toward adulthood. We all take side roads, which veer off into misbehavior, minor or major, depending on your standards. Our role as good parents is to guide our children back onto the main path as often as is necessary.

We direct them by discipline, which sometimes means punishment, but most of the time means guidelines or road markers for their life paths. Discussed first will be the negatives of punishment and anger. Then will be the upbeat ideas for reinforcing the acceptable behavior paths for a smooth trip on the road ahead.

No one likes punishment, not the one who has to think up the punishment and not the one who has to receive it. But certain misbehaviors demand punishment. Since each family has different standards, do what is right for you. However, if you feel tense about all the negative behavior, play "**Limit My Nos**" with the children. You tell them "No" only in extreme cases. Reword your thoughts in the positive. Instead of saying "No radio playing tonight," say "Let's have radio playing for fifteen minutes tonight." You have thereby met your need to have some quiet time. You have also met their need to listen to music.

You might as well be negotiators rather than be at odds with one another. You are different people with different needs, but you are living in a family. So you must work together to solve problems.

A child has a right to make a mistake, but there are good mistakes and bad mistakes. You have to decide when to punish. We never punish for accidents. Once when we were at a restaurant, my daughter spilled her orange juice. My husband said, "Accidents happen. Let's clean it up." It was nothing special to us. That is what we usually say. But a lady from the next table turned around and said, "I overheard what you said to your daughter and was very impressed. I only wish more parents would treat their children like people and not yell at them." My daughter was so happy with the lady's reaction that she felt like spilling her juice again.

In a case like this one, punishing won't do anything except lower the child's self-esteem. Her mistake of knocking over the juice happened. What needs to be done is to clean it up. But if she doesn't start to clean it up right away, then that is certainly a mistake, and we can discipline for that.

What makes a good punishment? It has to be the logical consequence of the problem. It has to fit the crime. It has to be swift like your saying in the car that they can't talk for the next three red lights. It has to clear the air. If you spill the juice, it is an accident and you don't get punished for that. If you don't try to clean it up, however, your punishment is that you can't have any more juice for that meal. The next meal we will start over fresh and clean with no recitals of past indiscretions. Logical, fitting, swift.

You also have to decide in misbehavior problems who owns the problem. This concept of ownership, made popular by Dr. Thomas Gordon in *Parent Effectiveness Training*, I have modified to fit my familial needs. If your child spills the juice, it is his problem. He needs to clean it up. If he doesn't and the juice remains on the floor and the table, then it becomes your problem. Its being there bothers you, not your child. But since it is his responsibility, you need to administer a reminder or finally a punishment. Or you can clean up the spill yourself, solving your problem. But the time will come when you can't face another spill and when he is old enough to take responsibility for his actions. Then you both own the problem. If, after you have discussed with him both sides of the issue, he still doesn't reach for the sponge immediately, then it is your cue to administer the punishment.

Different "crimes" demand different punishments. If you can't think of one that is logical, you can fall back on the multi-purpose ones. For younger children, one that works well and is used in many nursery school classes is the time-out chair. This method is especially appropriate when the youngster is emotionally overloaded. He may just need some quiet time to get himself together. Also, he won't like the lack of attention being paid to him. He won't need to stay in the time-out chair for long. Since he probably doesn't have much of a concept of time, you can allow him back into civilization when you see that he has made an effort to become human again. Variations on the time-out chair are the time-out corner and going to a different room, my personal favorite because it gives him a small sense of being able to make his own decision and doesn't make him associate a certain area with punishment. Going to his room is my least favorite, because his room should be a place of love and positive strokes. Often you can give him two choices. He can stop the misbehavior, or he can go to a different room.

Be flexible in deciding which punishment to give. What fits one crime may not fit another, and what fits one child may not work for another.

You should also be flexible about misbehaviors. Play **"I Thought of a Better Way to Handle It."** Try something creative like "I want to see the floor of your room by 6:00." Or "you have to learn the capital of California before you can join us again." Often you will feel better when you say, "I am really disappointed that you did thus and so. Let's try harder not to let it happen again."

73

Separate their actions from them. After a flare-up, be sure to say, "I still love you, even though I can't stand what you did." You like them. You don't like what they did or the fact that they keep doing it over and over again. By the same token, when he yells, "I hate you," what he really means is "I don't like what you did." He is entitled to his feelings, however negative or hateful sounding they may be. But he is responsible for his actions and for complying with the standards of the family and the situation.

For older children, you may want to restrict some activities as a punishment. You should both work out a hierarchy of punishments so that you in the heat of the moment don't blurt out, "Since you didn't put away the dishes tonight, you can't go anywhere for a month." Play **"Make the Punishment Fit the Crime."** Give them a say in what possible punishments there will be. Then they will know what to expect. If for any reason you or your spouse have given a punishment that you later realize is inappropriate and after a conference between the two of you, you have decided that a mistake was made, admit it. Play **"I Can Make Mistakes, Too."** Say, "I made a mistake. I was so angry that I gave out too harsh a punishment. Instead, this is what your punishment should be." What will probably happen is that your child will say, "I was also wrong, and I'm sorry." Those last seven words can be very hard for any age person to say. But they are so often necessary. If you have trouble admitting that you are wrong, play, **"I'm Wrong, and You Are Right."** Practice to yourself saying that expression over and over until you feel comfortable enough to say it in public. The first time is the hardest. After that, you will be more free with your apologies and so will those around you. No one is perfect. But we all can be fair and caring.

Children's behavior in public can sometimes cause you to feel embarrassment. For example, if you are in the market check-out line and your child starts acting up, you feel embarrassed that the others in the market see his behavior and think that you aren't a good parent. First of all, remember that if they are parents, they have been in the same circumstance before and will be again. If they aren't parents, they will be in your shoes of embarrassment at some time, and then they will understand. What you should do is play **"Divertimento."** Divert him into some other behavior. If he is little enough to be in the seat in the cart, take him out and hold him. His body literally may be aching from sitting on the hard seat for so long. Dance with him. Sing with him quietly. Older children can help you unload the cart or count the people in line or look at the pictures of the animals on the dog and cat food bags. You can launch into a story called **"Malcolm, the Market Monster"** who misbehaves in the store. They will squeal with delight at the antics you dream up for them. You can play **"Divertimento"** in any place, especially in the homes of friends, restaurants, and places where children need to be quiet. Then people will wonder why your children are so well behaved. You can answer, "No, they are not sedated. They are just diverted." Now you may ask, "Why do I have to entertain them? Why can't they just sit or stand quietly?" The answer is that they are children. They do not, nor should they, have the same attention span adults have. It probably wasn't their idea to go to the market or friend's house or restaurant in the first place, either. They are playing at your activity now. Remember how bored you can get when you have to play one of their childish games when you are not in the mood? Draw your own parallels.

Another important game to play is **"Public Voices."** There are many times in public places when you need to remind them to use their public voices, that is, quieter voices. Instead of your constantly telling them to be quiet, which is not what you really mean, you can now casually remind them to speak more quietly.

The constant companion to misbehavior is anger on the part of both of you. Anger exists. Don't deny it, and don't let the children deny it. Anger kept inside and not allowed to be released turns on you as physical or emotional illness, neither of which you need. Parent and child need to say, "I am angry!" You may want to talk about it then or wait until you have calmed down. I usually say, "I am so angry that I am ready to explode." When my children hear that line, they know they had better start behaving. I used to scream at them.

That technique works for many people. But I realized that I was getting a sore throat and didn't feel any better after I screamed. So I started to play **"Take a Deep Breath."** I would tell them that I was angry. Then I would take five or ten or thirty (depending on the extent of my anger) deep breaths similar to the long cleansing breaths associated with prepared childbirth. I literally would be blowing off steam and calming myself down at the same time. (The same technique works well for a child to calm down from a tantrum. He can't cry when he is blowing out his breath.) I also stopped screaming in the car the day I decided that the only way to get them to stop screaming at each other was not for me to scream back at them, but for me to turn up the car radio as loud as it would go. At first, the noise scared them, and they stopped their annoying behavior. As they got used to the technique, they began to laugh at the silliness of it, and their laughter would break the tension.

In the chamber of horrors through which children can put us daily, we need outlets for our anger, stress, and depression. These outlets will protect our sanity. Besides saying that you are angry and realizing that you are entitled to be and taking long, deep breaths, try the following: hit a pillow or punching bag, engage in some physical exercise like jumping jacks or running up and down the steps four times, find something that will make you laugh. Laughter releases certain chemicals in your brain. Your mood will change, and then you can decide if you want to solve the problem or ignore it. These outlets work equally well for your children's anger.

Also, you can make an agreement with a friend that when the bad times begin, you can call each other to commiserate and find dry land with a sane voice in the erratic sea of child rearing. A friend and I used to call each other during the 5:00 p.m. Arsenic Hour, knowing full well that we would hear the same amount of child whining and rowdiness on both ends of the line. But, because we were together for part of the time over the phone, we could survive during this time of day. Why, you may ask, did we spend the time on the phone ignoring our children when, if we were to spend time with them, they probably wouldn't be misbehaving? I am convinced that no matter how hard you try to engage them in activity, at certain times of the day or during certain developmental stages, they just will go "berserk." You first try to change the mood or divert their attention or channel their energies. If, after you have tried all these tactics and they still want to do it their way, you might as well let them. This acquiescence is another method for handling their behavior and is sometimes better than your being miserable, upset, or angry.

The point is that they will change their moods when they are ready. When a pre-teen or a teen slams his door in anger or lets off some steam by reiterating all the mean things you have done toward him, let him. Those are non-destructive methods he has to let out his anger. Children do not carry grudges as long as we do. In a few minutes or later that day, they are over and done with their bad mood. They may be ready for a cuddle or a ride somewhere. The problem is we adults may still be angry about the blow-up. Again, it is a matter of adjusting our timetable to be closer to theirs. It is fine to be honest and say, "I can't speak now. I'm still too angry." But they forgive and forget faster than we do. Let's beat them to the making-up some of the time. The bottom line for children is that they want to be loved. They want to do the right thing, but since they aren't adults yet, they proceed by trial and error, with satisfactory and unsatisfactory behavior, until they learn what we have been trying to teach them.

You would be surprised at how much they do absorb, even if they don't demonstrate it all the time. Just ask their friends' parents how they behaved when they had dinner at the other's home. That parent will describe your child as being polite, kind, warm, and helpful. Yes, this is the same child who doesn't seem to remember to clear his dinner dishes from your table. This brings me to the **"Trade a Child"** game. My husband has a theory that we would all enjoy parenting more if we would send our children to their friends' homes and take in the friends for alternate weeks. Since this would be done on a rotating basis, you would have your own child every few weeks, but he would be so confused as to whose home it was that he would behave as well in your home as he would in the home of a friend! Well, it is a thought.

Another suggestion for dissipating your anger is to take a **"Parent Break."** I am all in favor of parents taking vacation away from the children when they feel it is necessary or desirable. In fact, I always hope that when I go to my doctor with something wrong with me, she will say that the only cure is a week in the Bahamas. But she never does. So I prescribe the less radical **"Parent Break."** Say, "I can't get anything done now," (or "I can't stand it anymore" or any of the other countless comments we make during the day) "so I am going to take a parent break. I'll set the timer for ten minutes (or four years). While it is ticking, I can't be disturbed unless you see blood or vomit. When the bell rings, I will come out of my room and be pleasant and relaxed." You are entitled to time on your own, but with young children especially, you may need to structure it in this manner.

Thus far, we have dealt with punishment and anger. Now it is time to turn to the more optimistic realm of discipline. How can you and your children agree on what is proper procedure and discipline so that you can all live together harmoniously?

When a symphony orchestra plays a concerto harmoniously, the different instruments do not always follow the same notes. Some instruments play the harmony, some the theme, some the discordant sounds. Even the instruments are different and have solos at different times. But they are all working toward the same goal of producing music. It is the same with a family. You are all different, play different melodies, and have different feelings. But you are all part of the orchestra of life and should be making beautiful music together.

As the conductor gives the orchestra stability and structure, so should the family council supply the stability to your family discipline. The idea of a family council, made popular by Dr. Rudolf Dreikurs, stresses a democratic council. I feel that families aren't democracies, that the parents are the bosses, but even so, the children should be important influences in the decision-making process. Therefore, I recommend a modified family council, which works in the following way.

When any family member has a problem or an issue he wants

raised, he calls a family council. That person then explains the issue, and then each family member expresses his opinion or offers suggestions. The parents—or the children, depending on their ages—summarize the points raised. Any conclusions or new policies must be understood by everyone. In our version, the members don't have to agree, but they have to follow the conclusions.

This exercise is vitally important to the creation of a harmonious family arrangement. One of the major reasons that children get so frustrated is that they feel they have no control over their lives and no say in what happens to them. This modified family council gives them an opportunity to have their say and to influence the others in arriving at an outcome to their liking. But the final decision rests with the parents. Often at our family councils, we bring up issues about which we have no preconceived ideas, and therefore, we can agree completely with the conclusions the children propose. At other times, we have a good idea of what the conclusions should be. But we allow each child to express his feelings about the problem. Often we negotiate. Often we compromise. It is really fascinating to observe the family working together. When we have tears, we stop until enough tissues have been used and the person feels composed enough to speak.

One of the most common outcomes of our family councils is the use of a chart. This concept, widely used in the field of behavior modification, works very well for us all. One example is the use of the chart to help one of my daughters remember to bring home all her necessary homework supplies. Since we try to be positive instead of negative, she got a sticker on her chart each day that she brought home everything she needed for that night's homework. When she received ten stickers, she was able to get a treat. Treats range from a special hug, to staying up late one night, to not having to use the chart any more for that particular problem.

You can use the chart for practically anything, such as going to bed without a fuss, stopping the biting of nails, remembering to feed the pet, not pestering a sibling for an hour, returning library books on time, or wearing a bib during mealtime. Some cases call for the use of a negative chart. When we were having the problem of not being able to carry on a conversation without someone interrupting, we had a family council. The children had the idea to have a chart where they would get a bad mark any time they interrupted. They decided to compete with each other, and, in effect, monitored their own and each other's conversations until the problem resolved itself. After we stopped using that chart and the interruptions started to escalate, all we had to do was mention the idea of starting the chart again, and they calmed down.

Another method of harmonious discipline in which everyone has a say is the contract. Just be certain to write down all the parts of the contract and have the parties involved sign it. Make the contract short, simple, and practical. Once we used a contract for the book bag problem. My son wasn't packing up his book bag the night before, and so his mornings were chaotic as he searched for his belongings. After we discussed the problem together, we decided to make up a contract. If he packed up his book bag for seven nights, he would be able to watch a certain television program. I assumed he would carry out the contract in a week. It took him almost two weeks, but he did meet the requirements so he could watch his show. He also realized that it was a good idea to prepare the night before.

If a contract is an agreement between two people, then a bribe is merely an agreement that one person thinks up and imposes on another. I feel that contracts and bribes are closely related. Only semantics keeps them apart in polite society. In a family, they are both useful. "If you do this, I will do this" or "If you do this, I will give you this." Bribery is a form of compromise, and I recommend it highly. My only caution is that you should not make the reward of the bribe something expensive. You should use your imagination to think of your own list of "special family treats" comprised of things that are inexpensive and meaningful. One that works nicely for our family is the **"Squeezing Hug So Hard That Blood Will Shoot Out."**

You will find that when children have a say in what discipline they have, they will often be more strict than you ever were. They may also engage in bartering and other forms of working out problems with their siblings.

Since I recommend that you as parents not be dictators but be rulers of a semi-democracy, you will need to build up your arsenal to fight against three hated words: "That's not fair." You will probably go crazy if you try to make things fair. The simple fact is that life is not fair. Play **"Life is Not Fair"** by giving this realistic answer to the children. "Sometimes one of you gets something. Other times another one will. Other times nobody will. Some families have more material wealth than others, but no family has more love than yours." Make the best of what you have.

A good discipline game to play with children, starting with the very, very young is **"You Have a Choice."** When they misbehave say, "You have a choice. You can stop the whatever, or you can go to the time-out corner." This method gives them some small semblance of decision-making, even when they are behaviorally bankrupt.

Speaking of being bankrupt, when parents are emotionally bankrupt, they may hit their children. Hitting falls into three categories. One kind, a slap on the hand to a young child, is often interpreted as a reminder that something is unacceptable. At times like these, actions can speak louder than words. But a second kind, hitting out of anger, is done by parents at a time when it would be better for them to cool off first. Usually after you have slapped a child, you feel guilty. You were using an angry shorthand, but no matter how justified it seemed at the time, it probably only taught your child that you are bigger than he. When you feel the urge to strike, stop, stand back, and count to ten. Even let out a scream. When you have cooled down, play **"Reached the Limit."** Tell your child that you have reached your limit, that you are very angry, and that you need to decide how to handle the situation. The third type of hitting is the beating, which can only be classified as child abuse. If that is one of your techniques, stop immediately. If you can't, then get help from a local agency that specializes in this problem. You will help yourself and your offspring more than you'll ever know. An abused child may become an abusive parent.

What if the form of discipline you choose is not working? Change it. You might have to press that imaginary mood changer button or give an enormous hug to someone with whom you are very angry. Be inventive. That is your challenge. There is no right way to discipline unless what you are doing is working, and then it is wonderful. The best ally you have in the field of discipline is good communication among all of you.

You all need to talk about your feelings and emotions– both good and bad ones. It is important for children to realize that adults can feel afraid, tense, nervous, crabby, and furious. To emphasize this point, play **"What's My Emotion?"** Each family member acts out an emotion he has felt. The others guess what it is and when that person may have felt it. You can also think up situations and have your group decide which emotion would be appropriate.

Another vital method for good communication is to know how to be a good listener. As Dr. Thomas Gordon discusses in *Parent Effectiveness Training*, you need to know when to say "Sounds like you had a bad day" or "You sound upset about your friend." When you speak with non-judgmental words, you give your child the message that you are interested in hearing what he has to say. You have given him an opening. If he trusts that you will be a supportive—although not necessarily an agreeing—listener, he will communicate better with you. A common complaint among teenagers is "My parents don't listen to me." Well, now your child will not be able to say that and really mean it, because you will listen and let him vent. When the time comes for you to respond, or if you need to initiate a conversation, talk in ways that tell how you feel. Don't label him. An example is "You are a slob." A non-judgmental way to say the same thing without name-calling would be to say, "Your clothing needs to be put away before bedtime."

Play **"Mood Detector"** when your child is out of sorts. When you see that your child is acting more negative than usual, look for the cause. It could be that he is striking out at you because he feels inadequate on the sports field. Or maybe he has cheated on a test and is punishing himself by being mad at himself and the whole world.

Sometimes his mood can continue for days, but when you assure him that whatever he did probably isn't as bad as the punishment he has meted out to himself, he will be grateful to you. He will need extra reassurance that you love him no matter what and forever, and that all children have these kinds of moods. My children always felt much better when I told them that their behavior or misbehavior was age-appropriate and even written about in some psychology books.

Your children are not the only children who misbehave. You can get through the tense times with them if you keep in mind that they are just children and that you are all learning and growing together. Communicate openly, discuss, rule in a semi-democratic manner, and, in the really stormy times, reassure yourself that tomorrow will probably be better. My fantasy about harmonious discipline in families is to do away with the double edged sword of teenagers sitting in a rap session moaning about how bad their parents are and the parents at dinner parties decrying the situation concerning their misbehaving children. I want the two generations to sit together to discuss with each other how relations can improve. The glow from their conversations will light the path toward more compatible family living.

JACKET ALERT!

Chapter Seven:
Self-Esteem

Chapter Seven:
Self-Esteem

Put down this book for a few minutes. Make a list called **"Who I Am."** Write down at least ten nouns and/or adjectives. If you read on before you have done your list, you may never know your self-esteem quotient.

Now– if somewhere near the top of your list you have written the word "person" even coupled with words like "satisfied" or "wonderful" or "terrific," then you have a high level of self-esteem. Of course, you are pleased that you can put on the list that you are a husband/wife and parent, but you must remember first and foremost that you are a person, and a wonderful one at that.

Self-esteem, as I define it, is the ability to walk into a room of people with your shoulders back, standing tall, knowing that you have a great deal to offer those assembled. You have confidence in yourself and respect for yourself.

Your self-esteem evolves either because your parents instilled it in you or because you had an appreciative audience of friends and associates as you blossomed into the person you are. If you feel that your self-esteem level is not high enough, then as you do the following exercises with your children to develop their self-esteem, also do them for yourself. Your goal is to have your entire family stand tall on the foundation of self-esteem.

Everyone has the need to feel wanted and loved. Of course, you love your children and are doing everything you can for them. But you need to tell your children how you feel. To bolster their self-esteem, you should tell your children the **"Self-Esteem Creed"** each day, "You are your own person. I will love you forever, no matter what, just because you are you." Every day. Also, say the **"Estelle List"** (named for my mother), "You are gorgeous, wonderful, talented, and caring."

Yes, some days you will be so angry with your children that you won't want to be on the same planet with them, let alone give them praise and support. But what you have to remember is that you are angry at them for what they did or did not do, not for the people they are. You should say, "I don't like what you did, but I do love you." Especially when the pressures of the world outside the family are overwhelming your child, he needs to be assured aloud over and over that you are on his side.

Researchers have proven that babies are individual from the time that they are born. You have observed the same principle by watching your newborn's reactions to life. Now you can guide that child within his environment, but he will always be his own unique person. If he will not be what we want him to be, we must learn to accept him for the person he is.

In the early months, we strive to meet his infant biological needs, but we also must stroke his emotional needs. As we touch his body, we give him pleasure. Soon, he will pass a maturational milestone and begin perceiving himself as a separate identity. His warm feelings develop into the unbridled love he feels when he translates those feelings into a true smile.

As he crawls and stands and conducts his baby scientific experiments, he longs to please you. When you respond with praise and hugs, he senses that he must be doing a fine job in his babyhood. When you smile at his first steps, you have both reached another milestone. He, of course, will never be the same. He literally sets foot on the course of wild exploration and moves away from you in tiny steps, then leaps and bounds, until he is completely independent as an adult. The milestone for you is that you felt pleasure when he accomplished something totally on his own. But remember, no matter what you did for him or to him, he didn't walk until he was ready. It is important for you to retain an understanding of this pattern throughout your parenting years. In other words, give him as much guidance as possible, but realize that his actions and reactions have to come from him as he proves his individuality. Then you praise the positive. Your job as a parent is to give support through all his "steps." For all his future accomplishments, you should duplicate the joy you felt when he first toddled.

As he continues to grow, play **"Have a Say in Your Schedule."** Ask if he wants you to cut the nails on his left hand first or his right. *He* wasn't given the choice about whether or not the nails should be cut. You decided that part. But if he can be an active participant in part of the project, his negativism factor shrinks.

Continue to be positive in your commands to him. When he is dragging his jacket on the ground, you have to decide which way to remind him about the proper behavior. A "Don't drag your jacket" with its negative tone translates to him as, "Oh, here is another thing you are doing wrong." This feeling can lead to low self-esteem. But if you take the second choice, you can be non-judgmental. Try to say instead, "Jackets can get dirty on the ground." He'll get the same message that he should pick up his jacket, but he will not feel so blamed for doing what a child does. However, a third choice is the best, because it takes the boosting of his self-esteem a step further. Make him a partner in deciding how to solve his jacket dilemmas. Say, "Jacket alert!" You have alerted him to the problem, and he will be able to think up his own solution. Your underlying message to him is that he can say "I can understand the problem and think of my own solution. I'm terrific."

When he arrives at the stage where everything is "by myself," congratulate yourself and commiserate at the same time. Since our goal is to have him become independent, whenever he does a task by himself, he is progressing well. But life must go on, appointments must be kept, and he is still trying to put on that sock. You can start his getting dressed a little earlier in the morning so you won't be late, or you can use your parental prerogative. "I know you like to get dressed yourself, but right now I have to be your helper, because I am in a hurry. Where are those toes, anyway?" You have validated his feelings, explained your need, and diverted his attention, all as you accomplished your goal of getting him dressed quickly.

Just plan enough other times when he can practice his dressing skills. He is bound to make mistakes, but remember that a mistake made in the learning process can be labeled a good mistake. Putting on his shirt inside out is a good mistake. He has mastered all the skills necessary in shirt-putting-on except one– hiding the seams. He will eventually learn how to play **"Seam Magician,"** making the seams disappear. But in the beginning, he may be so proud that he has put on his shirt, that his self-image is more important than wearing the shirt the right way that day. By the way, many nursery school teachers enjoy seeing children arrive dressed less than perfectly. They know that these children are receiving good home training in doing things on their own.

In their efforts to accomplish, children certainly will fail. They need to know that failure is all right, that everyone fails at things. "Zippers sometimes take more than three tries before they work." "I sometimes have trouble pouring the milk, also."

Make audio or video tape recordings of their voices for two reasons: for immediate satisfaction and to listen to or to watch the tapes years later to help you remember the sound of their voices and some of their precious expressions. Another way they can look back on their development is for you to write them **"Linda Letters."** Linda Letters are named for my cousin Linda who gave me the idea years and letters ago. Since her name means "lovely" in Spanish, the name for the letters is even more fitting. These letters should tell the "lovely" things your child has done in each of the months of his first year and then every six months for the rest of your life. Whenever he reads them, he will have from you a present of your thoughts. His self-esteem will be boosted tremendously. My husband and I usually write the letters as a team. He will make the list of topics to be included. I will do the actual writing. He will proofread and make additions. Then we both sign the letters. We let them read the baby letters when they can read handwriting. Then we give the others to them each birthday and half birthday.

Gift giving from child to parent is another area where you can bolster self-esteem. Encourage children to make gifts for you. The cherished drawing, story, or piece of pottery can be much more meaningful than a store-bought gift. One of the best gifts can be a **"Promise Coupon"** given to you by your child. He can promise to do one of your chores or promise to take you to the park on a sunny day. When he can give a gift from himself, he knows that what he possesses inside of himself is worthwhile, that he is worthwhile. You can also reciprocate with a **"Promise Coupon"** for him. You promise to do one of his chores or take him to a ball game or read him seven books in a row.

Spend private time with each child each day. He will eventually realize that your time is precious, maybe because you have told him over and over for years. But he knows that when you can spend time with him, he must be important in your eyes. Sometimes, actions speak louder than words. Sometimes words speak louder than actions: "I love you forever, no matter what" every day. Also, let him overhear you saying wonderful things about him to others.

Encourage him to make his own decisions and his own learning mistakes as often as possible. Play **"Solve It Yourself"** where you tell him that you know he has the skill to solve the problem himself. This help in getting him to function from his own mind is a positive step anytime you do it.

Whenever their fears and anxieties need to be discussed, you can help to enlarge their self-esteem by creative story telling. Play **"Henry's Story Problems."** We use the adventures of a naughty cat named Wagga Wagga, first created by my father Henry. If your child is having trouble with an anxiety or a misbehavior, he may respond better by hearing about the problem through the detachment of an imaginary character. Wagga Wagga always disobeys and always misbehaves. His friends and family gently guide him back to correct behavior. The children love to hear about someone else who misbehaves. You can work out many of their problems through this creative storytelling. Also useful are puppet talks or stuffed animal talks where your child may attribute to this object something with which he is bothered. Together you, he, and the animal can solve what is on his mind.

Another way you can learn how he is feeling is by having a weekly **"What I'm Thankful For."** Each family member tells the things and people for which he is thankful that week. When you hear the sensitivity and understanding about life that comes out of their mouths during these sharing sessions, you will be amazed at what wonderful children you are raising. You too deserve to be patted on the back, because you are giving them an outlet to express their feelings. For equal time, you can have a **"Yuck Session"** where they can express what's bothering them.

One of the unwritten rules of childhood is that your children will rarely perform when you want them to. This is especially true when the audience is primed and ready to watch. You have a right to tell them in private that you felt disappointment and embarrassment when they didn't do what you asked them to in front of the guests. Ask them how you both should handle the situation the next time it arises. Come to an agreement to which both of you can adhere. In other cases of disagreement, criticize the action, not the child. The child is the one you will love, no matter what he has done. His action or inaction is what you need to address.

During the years when your child's emotions are running unbridled, his self-esteem needs to be boosted even more. It is very easy for you to show your love for him when he is on an upswing and having positive moods. But he needs you even more when he is in his terrible twos or fours or elevens and any other terrible number. Many a bad mood (his or yours) can be broken if you change the predictable patterns of yelling or brooding by reaching out for a hug or a good cry. During the moodiness, you can all play **"Not Feeling Alone"** in which you write down on strips of paper thirty descriptions of feelings like strong, weak, aggressive, dynamic, caring, and tender.

Put them into a hat, and take turns reaching for one and acting it out. The audience has to guess what feeling it is and when he last felt it. It is important for your upset child to know that you, as an adult person, can also feel upset or scared or guilty about things. When you acknowledge your vulnerabilities, your child will realize that his fears and anxieties are normal and that he doesn't need to be guilty about having these feelings. He'll stand taller now that you have lifted the weight of guilt from his shoulders. His self-esteem will soar, and he may even smile in between the gloomy moods.

You can further boost your teenager's self-esteem by including him in your thinking process. Play **"I Have a Problem."** Say, "I have a problem. Will you help me think of a solution?" His reaction should be, "Wow, my parents must really think highly of me for them to want to know my opinion."

A very common complaint from teenagers is that they are afraid their friends will not like them. This is the time when they need a large dose of self-esteem. Play **"Royalty for the Day."** Your teen needs to believe in himself first, so that others will then believe in him. He will be king for the day, or she will be queen for the day. He will act as a king would act, knowing inside that he is as happy and proud as a king should be.

If you are told that your teenager and certainly all his friends think you are the worst person ever, play "**Hear What My Friend Has To Say.**" Arrange a lunch date with your teenager and one of your close friends. With only the two of them there, have your friend explain to your offspring why he or she is your friend and what qualities are special about you. Always reciprocate for your friend's teenager. Once your child realizes that those outside of the family world can find something right with you, he may feel better about introducing you to his friends.

A wonderful lesson you can teach your child, one that will forever make him feel good about himself, is how to be organized. How can you teach him how to be organized, you may ask, if *you* don't even know how to be? Well, just think how much better you would feel about yourself if you were more organized. Start slowly. Make a list of things to do. Tackle one part of one room. Find a place for each item. Stack papers into categories, then file away the piles in places you will remember. Make your kitchen more convenient by putting the things you need for a usual meal in one cupboard, so you only have to open one cupboard door for the whole meal. Don't let mail sit around unanswered for more than three days. That means twice a week is mail night. Stand in each room and ask, "Is this the best place for this?" If the answer is "no," then find a better place for it. Once you feel organized, stay that way. You will find that the day has more minutes in it, because you no longer waste time worrying about not being organized.

To organize your child, give him a set place for his schoolbooks, lunch box, backpack, jacket, etc. Set aside cubby space in a centrally located closet. When he comes home from school, all his things will go into his cubby. Then he'll know where to find the things he needs, and the morning departure will not be a free-for-all. Show him how to choose which homework should be done first, which last. Make sure he knows how to organize any composition or any report. Give him a set way that is easiest for him to practice his spelling words. Show him how to look up a word in the dictionary even if he doesn't really know how to spell it. No work seems overwhelming if you know how to attack it. Take the hardest step, and the rest of the work will flow from there.

Your child's self-esteem about his school work is largely determined by his teacher. If you are fortunate enough that he has a nurturing teaching, then for this school year, you can relax about his fragile ego. Your job as parents is to be supportive. All you can ask is that he do his best on his work. If his best gets him a C average, then you must accept that he is an average student. You can still love someone who is not the best in the class. He must know that you are behind him all the way, no matter what his grades are. If he is not doing his best, then you need to find out why by listening carefully to him and trying to see what is behind what he says is the problem.

Find some thing or things at which he excels, and give him ample opportunity to display his talents. Every child is gifted in some way.

You can be a **"Gifted Detector"** for your children and your friends' children. Be the one who spots a talent in the children. You will be bolstering the self-esteem of more people than you know. Being gifted is to a large extent a state of mind. If you feel you are gifted or that your child is gifted, you or he will probably act that way.

Self-esteem is feeling wonderful about yourself. You have to teach your children that they are wonderful. They need to know that they are like a king or queen inside, that they are capable of doing almost anything, that they can walk tall and be proud of their families and of themselves. Positive self-esteem is one of the most important gifts you can give to your child.

CREATIVE PLAY

Chapter Eight:
Creativity

Chapter Eight: Creativity

Your continual emphasis on creativity will enrich your child's life. His absorbent mind needs stimulation. As his first teacher, you must supply the necessary input to expand his intellectual horizons.

One of the synonyms for creativity is a pregnant imagination. And you thought you were done being pregnant! From the first time you are left alone with your newborn and he begins to cry, you will be called upon to deal with him creatively. How do you make him stop crying? Sometimes you bounce him up and down. Sometimes you make noises at him. Sometimes you stroke his forehead or his feet. Whatever you do, you use your creativity, that is, you search deep into your mind to find something to soothe him.

As your baby continues to develop, you sing with him, dance with him, and speak to him in different tones of voice. During this time of his life, he is sorting out noise, tone, texture, and images. Present him with an abundance of all these things. In his crib, you can change his patterned linen often. Rotate the mobiles above his head. Every other time you put him in the crib, place him with his head on the left side of the crib. You want him to be well-rounded, don't you? Remember Rule One: If he is all right, leave him alone. But when he needs a change of scenery, take him to a new corner of the room, or to a swing, or to a different, textured rug or mat. It is equally important for you to allow him to be held by many different people. Broaden his horizons. Expose him to many persons of different ages and to the variety of life.

As toddlers get older, stimulate them with toys. Toys have to be interesting, not expensive. Just because a toy is labeled "creative" doesn't mean you must buy it. Look for toys that are safe and age-appropriate for your child, not necessarily for what age is written on the box. You don't have to have hundreds of toys. Children often feel overwhelmed when they look around their toy areas. That is why you may hear: "I have nothing to do." Store some. Rotate them. The children certainly won't miss the ones you put in storage and will be delighted when you bring them out again.

Avoid sexual stereotyping when it comes to toys. When your son wants to play with a doll, that's fine. With it, he will practice his fathering skills and grow up to be a warm, loving husband and father. Similarly, when your daughter wants to push around a truck, let her use her imagination. Children need exposure to all sorts of activities to become well-rounded. Your job is to encourage, not discourage.

Parents divide themselves into two different groups when it comes to weapon toys. Those who are against them—and I number myself in that group— will find that there is not much you can do when your child takes a strategic bite from a sandwich and realizes that it now looks like a gun. So he'll proceed to shoot peanut butter and jelly. You can try to differentiate between shooting people and things, and you can try to re-channel his energies by asking, "What else can you think to make out of that sandwich?" But the shooting seems to be a stage related to their need to make themselves powerful in a world in which they are so little. The passage of time is probably your better ally in the war of the weapons.

So what are the best toys? They are the ones that keep the child's interest. Large motor and small muscle control can be stimulated by appropriate toys. Then later, mental games will become favorites. Basic house toys for the pre-school years should include: blocks, puzzles, crayons, blank paper and coloring books, books, tricycles, balls, pretend dress-up clothes, stacking toys, dolls, trucks, play dough, a small slide, a swing, simple board games, and stuffed animals.

During your child's toddler and pre-school years, you can develop numerous outlets for his and your creativity. Cook together, especially as a mood breaker. Play **"Hug Emergency"** where one of you yells, "I have a hug emergency" and the other one has to run from wherever he is to deliver an enormous hug. Begin **"Family Read-Alouds"** which you should continue throughout your lives. The sounds of the reader's voice, the rhythm of the words, the turning of the pages, the story itself, and the togetherness make this a meaningful way to share time.

Tell stories about them. Their attention will never wander as long as they are in the story. Tell **"Round Robin Stories"** where each person says a word or a sentence or a paragraph, continuing in a circle over and over until you all decide the story should end.

When you are telling stories, and indeed whenever you speak, use proper grammar. You want your children to speak and write with excellence. The examples you set influence them the most.

Other word games are enjoyable as well as educational. Play **"Homonyms."** Whenever someone says a word that has a homonym, call "Homonym," and ask your child what he thinks the other meanings are.

Play **"Similarity."** When two people come to breakfast wearing red shirts, call "Similarity," and ask your child what is similar. He may also see other similarities beside the red shirt. So give him extra credit with positive strokes of words and hugs.

Put on plays and talent shows. Give your child the imaginary setting or two characters to be used in the play. For wonderful stretching of the creative mind, play **"Three Object Play."** Find any three unrelated objects in the room. Tell your child he has five minutes to prepare a play using those three objects. This activity works especially well when friends are visiting, because it affords them structure as well as fun.

Similar to plays are **"Talent Shows."** No matter what talent or training you have had, you can have fun participating in a talent show. You can act a pantomime, do charades, sing songs, invent a dance, tell a story, or try to be a magician. The rules for a talent show are that each person must do something and that everyone should have fun. When your child performs in a non-threatening situation, he expands his self-confidence.

When should your child start to take extra-curricular classes? Many communities offer classes in art, music appreciation, gymnastics, and cooking for pre-schoolers. Proceed on the theory that it is a good thing to expose your children to many experiences. But don't overdo. Use your child's interest level, your time demands, and your child's developmental age as guides, not what the neighbors are doing or what you think you should do to be "good parents." I tried to limit our activities to two a week. Those who schedule children for something every day after school or for every evening should stand back and evaluate the schedule. Should your child be having more free, unstructured time? We are currently being warned about the problems evolving from the child who is hurried through his activities and his childhood. Your child may thrive on a full set of classes, or he may function better with a few, coupled with a large dose of free time. You and your child are the best judges.

One of our favorite activities is Suzuki music lessons. My children have played the violin since they were four years old and, like most other Suzuki students, play for hours by memory, feel a great deal of self-confidence, and love to perform. The technique relies on the parent as teacher between the lessons, the constant listening to the music, and much positive reinforcement.

More traditional music lessons of any kind are also enriching, but the tension of the practice time can defeat the purpose of the enjoyment. Play **"Practice is Your Responsibility"** and mean it. Have the child meet with his teacher and decide what length of time is expected. It will be his responsibility to do the practicing. Not everyone was meant to play an instrument, but everyone should be given the opportunity to be exposed to one.

Let your child sample what is available in your neighborhood. Make him well-rounded by engaging him in mental and physical activities in non-pressuring ways. He is only a child once and is entitled to play often, but there is enough time in the day and in the week to supply him with structured, interesting samples of life's wonders.

More creativity can be stimulated by looking in your back yard. Play **"Nature Sounds."** Everyone should be very quiet. Then listen to all the nature sounds. Guess where the birds are going, what the squirrels are doing, why the bees make noise. Transport yourselves to the jungles when you hear the truck's brakes screech like an elephant's roar.

Be **"Flower Detectives,"** and count all the red flowers or group them into categories with one of you counting the roses, the other the daisies.

Make your walk into **"Treasure Hunts on the Ground."** Bring a bag or basket, and pick up interesting items along the way. On one walk, my son and I found three sticks, two smooth pebbles, one large, jagged rock, two pieces of plastic, a receipt, and a penny. When you return home, you can continue your game. Play **"Organize the Treats."** Put them in size order. Group them by color. Mix them up in random order. Take one away, and try to guess which is missing. Make up a story about them. Stretch your minds. Enjoy the give and take of imaginations.

Another good source of creativity revolves around food. Children of any age can play in the kitchen. Sometimes you may even be able to eat the food. From letting your toddler make celery people to letting your teenager make a full course meal, you will have treats year after year. You can surprise the whole family with a picnic in your back yard in the summer or even in the snow. Or make a Hawaiian luau on the coldest day of the year.

Children should be involved in planning their birthday parties whenever they show interest. Birthdays are a major topic of conversation around our house, so much so that we had to make a rule that the children could think about their birthday parties to themselves, but that we couldn't start making the actual plans until two months before. Keep the outline of the party simple. Guests arrive, play age-appropriate games, and go home with a goody bag or gift. I don't allow the children to open presents while the guests are here. It is very difficult for a young child to sit around watching some other child open gifts and gifts and gifts. Also, I am a firm believer in "re-gifting" gifts my children don't want, so it is better to open the gifts after the guests leave. What makes a birthday party special is that it revolves around a theme. You can choose almost anything– a story book character, a favorite hobby, a color, a shape. One of our favorite parties was a "dot" party. We asked the guests to wear polka dots. We played "Pin the Dot on the Nose" and had a dot treasure hunt on the playroom floor. We gave out dot candy and connect-the-dots activity books for the goody gift. Do what you can afford to do. If you decide to hire outside entertainment like a clown, you should keep in mind that some children are afraid when faces are covered with masks or make-up. If you decide to have a magician, ask him to gear his act to the attention span of the audience. Also, remember that while a clown or a magician may be a novelty in your home, other people may have used the same idea, and some of the guests will be seeing the third magician that month. Don't feel you must hire someone or go somewhere. Do keep the length of the party short, and vary the activities.

The party is not really over until the last thank you note has been mailed. As soon as your child can write his name, he should be responsible for signing and then later writing thank you notes for every gift he receives. This teaches him responsibility and manners and notifies the giver that the gift has been received. Don't make this writing a chore. Let him lick the stamps and close the envelopes. Work on them together, and talk about the people who came to the party as you write to each friend. The last part of the party for you is putting the photographs in his baby book or scrapbook.

More creativity abounds when you take trips with the family. Any trip is an adventure, whether it be to the grocery store or around the world. Your vacations with the children, which are by definition much different from vacations without the children, should be invaluable and enjoyable learning experiences for you all. We have gone to Europe with the children ever since they were two years old. People would say to us, "Why would you take them? They'll never remember anything." The point is to accentuate the positive. They do remember a great deal, and they enlarge their vocabulary and their conversational ability. The photographs reinforce what we have seen. You can find many inexpensive tours and lodgings. Choose the country that is a currency bargain that year. Here is a list of hints for your travels.

GUIDE TO ENJOYING TRAVELING
WITH THE CHILDREN

1. Make plans and reservations. You can't be free- spirits when you are traveling with the children.

2. After the effects of jet lag subside, keep them on their schedules as best as you can.

3. Have small children wear nametags with your address for that night written on them.

4. Each day, see a sight for your age and a sight for their interest level.

5. Tell them the history of the places.

6. Look for child-related places, like toy museums or parks.

7. Even though you are in strange beds each night, help them feel secure by doing your usual bedtime procedures.

8. Take many photographs with each of you in them.

9. Make many snack stops in the course of the trip.

10. Buy meaningful souvenirs. When you get back, your memories will be stimulated by the things you bring home.

11. Visit sights you read about in your pre-trip preparations. We read about a penguin parade in the Edinburgh Zoo in one of our children's books, so we made a point of watching the penguins marching when we were there.

12. Adults and children keep diaries in which you write or draw every night. The children's diaries are filled with illustrations of what they remembered from each day. These also serve as reminders for all of you. My daughter once left her trip diary on the airplane and was so upset that she wrote another one from memory.

13. Have each child carry an activity bag. Fill it with books, toys that can be played with on buses and airplanes, pencils, paper, their diaries, snacks, their jackets, and a change of pants (you never know what will happen).

14. Look for what is similar to where you live and for what is different.

15. Parents alternate days "on." One day you are the parent on duty. The next day your spouse is. This way, although you are with the children, you can feel that you are having a vacation as well.

16. Watch their faces as your children observe the breath-taking scenery, historical sights, and magnificent architecture. Then, if someone asks you why you bother to take the children, you'll be able to describe the wonder and pleasure. Tell them that you are making their geography and history books come to life. My children still point out Tudor architecture and topiary whenever they see it.

17. Children rally when they are on trips. Since the scenery is changing quite often, their interest levels are high. You'll see that they are much better behaved while they are on vacations. And if they do cry and carry-on, remember that they would have done so at home also, so you might as well be listening to the crying while you are sailing in the Aegean or looking at the Eiffel Tower. The benefits of traveling as a family far outweigh the inconveniences. At the airport once when we were returning to Washington, DC, from a trip to the British Isles, my husband and I were just congratulating ourselves on what a great job we did with the children on the trip. Then we saw a family with six children who were on the middle leg of their trip from Saudi Arabia to San Francisco. Inconvenience is relative, but being in a family of relatives makes you realize that the benefits are bountiful.

Whether you are traveling or not, you face the problems of eating in a restaurant. If it is the kind with waiters (who may also be called that because you have to "wait" for your food according to one of my children), you will need to think of creative ways to pass the time. Play **"World of the Restaurant Table."** Think of ten games you can play while waiting for the meal. Some of our favorites are **"Hide the Sugar," "I Spy," "Story about the Decor of the Restaurant,"** and **"Pass the Napkin"** (literally around in a circle until someone calls time when the one with the napkin has to say something silly). The best words to end the series of games are **"Hands in Your Laps"** because the waiter is on his way with the food. Your allies in a restaurant are the encouragement of the use of your restaurant voices, which are soft and polite, and their ordering from children's menus.

Creativity should stretch the mind, even bend it. As you have seen, I believe that you can be creative with anything. Take everything one step further, as long as your child's attention span allows. Don't stop after you have built with blocks. Make labels for your creation, and drive your toy cars up to visit the new city. Take any object, and play **"How Many Uses?"** Have your child think of unusual uses for it. Write down his ideas. Start with a drinking straw. He'll probably think of at least twenty different uses for it. We always say that we can keep the children occupied with a piece of string. No, not tying them up, but thinking of various uses for it.

Don't overlook your collection of stuffed animals. Certainly, they can play **"Stuffed Animal Party."** Seat the animals in a circle, and choose the animal whose special day it is. Or transform your room into a pet store with each animal on display.

Children should be taken to matinees of operas, plays, concerts, and ballets. Their cultural education rests on your shoulders. If *your* shoulders need broadening, do so as you broaden *their* minds. Discuss the stories or compositions in advance. Give them some high spots to expect. You don't have to like everything you see, but you need to be exposed to what is available.

When you take children to museums, you can have them play

"Art Curator" by telling them that they may pretend to choose five paintings to be put on display in their private, pretend gallery. As they walk through the art museum, they then will have a goal and may not feel overwhelmed at all they see. In other kinds of museums, you can play **"Find the Star of the Exhibit"** where you take a quick glance at what is on display. They then have to guess what you had in your mind. In the meantime, they will be looking at the exhibit without complaining. Time also passes very quickly in the children's museums and the "hands-on" exhibits.

No matter how much you prepare children for what they might see, be ready for surprises. Once, my daughter stood in front of an Indian display and recited all she had learned in school about that tribe. Some years before, she had been taught an art unit in nursery school. The teacher carefully described and had them duplicate, according to their own abilities, an abstract, a landscape, a portrait, and pointillism. On our next trip to the art museum, she ran up to each painting and told what genre it was. Everything was fine, until we rounded the corner. There in front of us was a nude. She shouted, "Look, she doesn't have on her clothes!"

Reinforce your outings by having the children draw or write about their experiences on the next occasion when you need a project for them to do. Hang the art on your specially designated art wall, and make a collection of their stories to give them when they are older.

You have in your mind an enormous wealth of creative ideas to share with your family. When you find that you have trouble getting those ideas out, you may want to be stimulated by looking at the creative sections of textbooks the children bring home. Or read some books dealing with creative approaches to life.

Your tasks as creative parents of a creative child are many. You need to expose him to the many aspects of life. Challenge him to think further than he would. Find interesting facets of, and uses for, a twig, a blade of grass, a piece of paper. Take cues from him, and stretch his mental boundaries. In the beginning, you are his window in the airplane of the world. Before you know it, he will be on his own mental plane, soaring into higher realms of creativity and enjoyment.

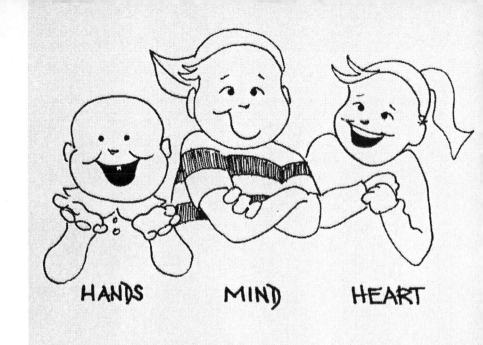

HANDS   MIND   HEART

Chapter Nine: Children's Rights & Responsibilities

Chapter Nine: Children's Rights & Responsibilities

If, as the expression says, our job as parents is to provide our children with roots and wings, then we have to pay as much attention to the wings as we do to the roots. We are all cognizant of the heritage we give to our offspring. We retell stories of relatives and discuss our backgrounds often. We are comfortable with the idea that children should know their roots and hope that they are firmly planted in our familial circle. But we parents have a harder time admitting what it means for children to have wings.

As our children win the battle of maturity, they have to separate from us by degrees. They are not part of us. They are separate, complete individuals learning how to live on their own. From the moment the infant first attempts to lift his head, he is starting to do things on his own. The next step is when he can balance on his elbows. Then come the rocking, the crawling, the walking. The terrible twos, terrible sixes, terrible fourteens, and all the terrible teen years (or whatever age you care to insert here) are all terrible because the child is asserting himself, trying to be his own person, stretching his wings.

If you view the terrible ages as a disagreeable but necessary stage in your child's development, you might be able to live through these periods with a little more compassion and a little more peace of mind. Just as you should not try to argue with or punish a toddler while he is having a tantrum, neither should you try to reason with a pre-teen or teen when he is in a foul mood. It is the child's job to strike out on his own, and if he has to accomplish it at the moment by having a tantrum or a screaming fit or a sulking mood, you need to step back for a while. The time to discuss the unacceptable behavior is after the blow-up, no matter who has done the exploding.

Yes, all children behave in an obnoxious manner at some time. They would be abnormal if they did not. You may be amazed when, after your child has visited with friends, you hear from the parents of the friend how well-mannered and well-behaved your child was. Are they talking about your child, the one who refuses to hang up his jacket, the one who has not said "thank you" without prompting in the last four years? Yes, your lectures about manners and proper behavior really did sink in.

However, even though the misbehaviors are part of the child's growing up, he still has responsibilities in the family. I have divided them into three categories– those he must do with his hands, those he must do with his mind, and those he must do with his heart.

Those responsibilities a child must do with his hands are tangible and obvious. The chores you assign him or the ones to which he agrees after a family council are either personal or family assignments.

A child must take care of his personal hygiene. From the time you no longer have to dress him or bathe him or brush his teeth for him, he is expected to be clean and properly attired for each occasion. If you find that you are dissatisfied with his choice of clothes or are tired of the morning clothing argument, you have the right to explain your problem. Remember that it is your problem, not his. A possible solution might be that he will be able to wear what he wants every other day or you get to choose for him each Wednesday. Maybe you both should go through the drawers and closet to weed out the clothes you all can no longer stand. This system works especially well for a child who is the recipient of hand-me-downs he hates.

Keep in mind that at different ages, different standards apply. It is perfectly fine to allow a nursery school child to go to school in pants that are inside out. If he puts it on himself, his self-esteem is more important than his fashion look. Later on, when the right clothes become so important, you and your child have to decide what your approach will be, taking into consideration your finances, your child's need to belong, and your closet space. Your child's peers have a keen sense of clothing etiquette. They know when someone is "out of it," and they know when someone overdoes the wearing of "in" clothing. Try to develop a balance as you remember some of the styles you wore when you were growing up.

The other personal hygiene responsibilities that your child has center in the bathroom. In the beginning, baths are a wonderful time for fun, exploration, and relaxation. When your child enters the "I like the dirt on my body" stage, the tub or shower is no longer user-friendly. This is when you need to set up a shower schedule to which your child must adhere. Daily inspections of teeth and fingernails are well within your rights. One day—and it may come without the slightest notice— your pre-teen or teen may become a showerholic. When you receive your next water bill, you may decide to have a discussion about setting a time limit on showering.

The hairbrush is one of those objects that may be covered with dust from disuse if your child has his true wish. But his responsibility is to make use of it as often as you both agree. Who should decide how your daughter wears her hair? In the beginning, of course you can. When it is no longer your decision, she will let you know. But there are those special occasions when you have a right to expect her to wear it in a certain style. These times should be discussed well in advance.

Then out of the clear blue, the day will dawn when your child will spend hours on his or her hair. This preening is his right, and he will probably never be satisfied with how his hair looks or with how he looks for that matter. It does not make any difference how much you have built up his good body image. During these teen years, he puts that information on the back burner of his brain. He has a right to complain about how the other kids are all better looking or how they all stare at him because he is so ugly. He is struggling with his personal image, much as a sculptor molds a piece of clay. Before that statue is finished, it will undergo subtle as well as obvious changes. The same is true with your child. Eventually, he will be "finished," and if you have done well in promoting his self-esteem, you will have given him a good foundation. Like the statue, he will be a masterpiece.

Another category of responsibility he has to do with his hands is chores around the house. Even a toddler should be expected to have some set jobs to do. He can put the napkins in the napkin holder, set the spoons on the table, or help you put away any twelve toys from the playroom floor. When he spills the crayons from the box, you should say to him, "It is your responsibility to pick them up. Let me hear them fall into the box." By using words like "responsibility" and "chores," you begin to teach your toddler important life patterns. If you can make them seem more like games, the concepts shouldn't have such disagreeable connotations.

The number of chores and their level of difficulty of course depend on the child. But choosing which chores to do and motivating him to do them are real challenges. Some families assign chores by ages of the siblings. Some draw pieces of paper from a hat to determine who does what that week. If you find that you have to remind him constantly to do his chores, something is wrong. You need to sit down to discuss "your" problem, and it is only your problem. You are the one who needs the chore to be done. But since it is his responsibility to do it, you need to have a meeting of the minds.

Sometimes a motivational chart helps. Each time a chore is completed, he gets a star or a sticker. After so many are on the chart, maybe he can have a break from doing that particular chore for a day. But because it is a chore, it has to be done eventually. Often, children balk at having to do things because they have no real say in the matter. So often, they have very little control over their lives. Therefore, the more you can involve them in deciding who does what and when, the easier the chores may become.

The chore of cleaning one's room is an interesting topic. Whether your child shares a room or has one of his own, he should be responsible for how it looks. *He* should be. It should not be your worry as long as the Health Department would not bar the door. You have a right to demand that you be able to see the color of the floor when it has to be swept or vacuumed and that the room meet mutually acceptable standards when guests visit, but at all other times, it is his domain. If he wants to keep the bed unmade or litter the floor, why not let him? This area is the only one over which he has complete control. The other rooms in the house presumably meet your cleanliness standards, so just have him close his door so you don't have to look in. You'll be surprised that he will decide eventually that he needs to tidy up.

The allotment of kitchen chores differs in each household. Keep in mind that a chore is neither masculine nor feminine. If you reap the advantages of living in the house, you have to do the chores that the house requires. If everyone shares in the jobs equally, then the problem of sexist stereotyping need not exist.

Their responsibility of handling money begins with their allowance, a topic on which everyone has his own opinion. How much should be given? Should it be withheld as a form of punishment? On what can it be spent? I feel that since things in this world cost money, and a child has no other way to acquire money, he should be given an allowance. It should be given just for existing. If you also want to pay him for jobs like babysitting a sibling or helping with the laundry, then that is extra money. But the allowance should be his to have. He will learn how to save and how to spend. He will count his money over and over. He may buy whatever he wants with that money as long as it is not used for something illegal or against the rules of the house. We use a three-part system for dividing the money. After our children have saved a certain amount of money, they put some in the bank, give some to charity, and use the rest as they see fit. We never withhold the allowance as a punishment, because we try, hard as it may be, to have the particular punishment fit the crime of the moment.

It is their money, so they should be allowed to spend it on whatever they want. When they are older, you will have to decide on a clothing allowance, that is, how much of your money they will be allowed to spend on clothes. But any of their own money can augment your limit. They can learn many lessons on the value of saving by themselves for something important when they have to manage their own allowances.

How older children can earn extra money by working on age-appropriate jobs can be a very maturing experience. I think children should be paid for babysitting their siblings. If they were not available or were not old enough, you would have to pay someone anyway, so why not pay them? Both girls and boys should be taught how to be good babysitters by you or by classes given in local community centers. When a pre-teen or teen does babysit, he has the responsibility to give full attention to those in his care. He should not merely "sit" around. Perhaps the word "babysitting" is not the best description. Maybe it should be called "baby-engaging," because the sitter should engage the children in activities that are age-appropriate, safe, and fun. The sitter has the responsibility to write down the agreed upon date on his calendar and on the family calendar and to be ready at the appointed time. At the end of the evening when the parents return, the babysitter has an obligation to report on what happened. And this speech should be made in multi-syllabic words rather than nodding or answering "yes" and "no" to the questions posed by the parents. The adults have a right to know what happened during the evening.

Just as boys should be encouraged to babysit, so should girls be encouraged to mow lawns in the neighborhood. I have always been bothered by the fact that the person who mows the lawn can charge sometimes as much as three times more than the one who babysits. So, girls, wake up and mow. And both girls and boys, learn how to babysit so you can practice your parenting skills before you have your own children.

There are many responsibilities for the child who is being babysat. He must behave within reasonable limits. The child should be told before the parents leave where the parents are going, when they will return, what he is allowed to eat, when his bedtime is, and that he will be missed. Since children fluctuate in and out of the "hating the sitter" stages, you have to remember that you have a right to go out. Maybe you can suggest a particular game or activity he can do with the sitter to ease his discomfort.

The next major category of children's responsibility has to do with what their minds produce. This includes schoolwork and homework, manners, and privacy.

A child has a responsibility to go to school. Even in his younger days when he says he does not want to go to nursery school, you need to tell him that he must go. As he matures and begins to have homework in elementary and then even more in secondary schools, he will go through stages of wanting to do the work and of not wanting to do it. Your job as a nurturing parent is to help him develop study skills that will have him organize his work, do things in priority order, and feel a sense of pride in his accomplishments even before they are graded. He is to do his best, while you must accept that his grades might be lower than you would like them to be. He is his own person with his own abilities. If his grade on a project is not as high as you wanted it to be, that is something you will have to accept. If he did his best, that is all you can ask.

However, if he is not working up to his potential, you need to be a detective and investigate what the problem is. Sometimes it is in the home. Sometimes it is because the teacher is not nurturing your particular child, even though everyone else in the school loves that teacher. Maybe the chemistry between them is not there. Maybe the problem is with the developmental stage of your child.

While you are looking for the problem and when you discover what it is, try to have patience. Your child, although he may not act that way, really is upset that things are not going as well as they should. With all the stress-provoking elements bearing down on him, his frustration and depression levels can overwhelm him. He needs you to help him solve his problem or to reassure him that his blue period will be over soon. You don't know when that will be, just that it will be soon.

Homework rules must be established by both of you. Whether or not you allow him to play for a while before he works, he must know when he is expected to begin. You must provide him with a quiet, comfortable place to do his work. Keep in mind that some teenagers actually work better with music or television blaring. But do establish a set time and place for your child to work. Around the age of ten, when he has a strong need to be at the hub of the family activities, it may be wise to allow him to work near the family.

Many schools have instituted the policy of having the students write down all the homework assignments. That is a good way to keep informed about what is due and when. But homework is not your responsibility, nor should it be your work. Of course, you may help in solving a problem or finding a country on the map, but you are not the one who is being graded. You will be establishing a helpful lifetime habit by teaching your child to proofread (even though he will tell you that no one else ever does it). If he proofreads by himself, his work has to be better.

If he does not do the homework, it is his problem, not yours. If this situation becomes a habit and his grades begin to drop, then you do need to enter into the problem.

His book bag needs to be packed up and put in the designated spot before he goes to bed at night. That way, when he has to hurry off in the morning, he and you will not have to go on a hunt for the essentials.

The schooling process is such a main part of your child's life. But, during the days and periods when he is having a hard time either academically or emotionally, you must be on his side. He may need an extra hug, a special time out with you, or a temporary break from his workload. When he is having trouble, show you understand by listening and responding. The stress he can feel at these times is very real to him. Indeed, it can seem overwhelming. You can ease some of this pressure by helping him to list the work he has left to do. A simple list in front of him might not seem as overwhelming as looking at his big stack of books. I also recommend a study skills course which teaches your child how he learns– that is, by seeing, hearing, writing, or moving. Then he can use specific methods for his own improvement. Remember, never overlook the power of a giant hug and kiss when he is low.

The next area of responsibility over which a child has control is that of manners. And he does have control. For many years, it seemed to me that my children acted as though they couldn't say "thank you" until I said, "What do you say?" Of course, I set examples by being polite myself, but they seemed to be on their own time schedule. Whenever your children do show good manners, use positive reinforcement.

Further social graces all have to be taught when the children are at the right age. When they are ready to answer the telephone, they need to be told what you want them to say. You also have to remember that just because you are a parent, you cannot forget your telephone manners. If the person to whom you are speaking is not a parent of young children, he might not understand when you ask him to wait a moment while you tend to your toddler. Before I had children, I resented the fact that I had to be on hold while the person on the other end was dealing with his or her child. It wasn't until I had to do the tending in my home that I realized that if the phone rings while the children are awake, there is the chance that I will be needed away from the phone.

Reciprocating visits becomes very important. In the early years, you are the one who does the inviting of the playmates and their parents, but if you have been a good teacher, your older child will know that after he has been to a friend's home, he should invite that person to his. That way, your child will learn how to be both a guest and a host or hostess.

Table manners differ from house to house. Make certain your child knows how to eat at both casual and formal meals. You don't want to be embarrassed in someone's dining room someday when your child says, "Look at all these forks at my place!" Sometime before you go to such an affair, you and your child together should set a full place setting. Explain for which course each piece of silverware is used.

Other table manners include where the napkin should be during a meal, when to start eating, and how to be excused from the table. The talk at a family meal should be an exchange of ideas, a sharing of the day's activities, or anything else that is pleasant. Mealtimes are not discipline times, nor should they be a time for negativism from anyone. I also suggest rotating the seating arrangements so everyone has a chance to be at the head of the table or seated next to another person. Just because someone is the third-born or the oldest, why should he get to sit in any certain seat? When you come to the point when your mealtime runs smoothly, all the family members will look forward to being at the table together.

Also under the heading of manners falls social lying, sometimes called the "white lie." Children must realize that there are times when they will be called upon to tell a social lie. They have to learn how to distinguish between protecting the feelings of others and looking at the situation as a whole. Then they will know when the right time is to say what the other person wants to hear. Your child certainly will overhear you tell a social lie. You can only hope that he is mature enough to wait until you two are alone before asking you why you lied. Quite simply, there is a time to lie in social situations. But there is a more important time to tell the truth. It is the responsibility of both of you to set up guidelines as to when the truth should be foremost.

When children are speaking to adults, they have a tendency to avoid eye contact and to mumble. Part of the social graces that they have to be taught is successful communication. They need to be shown how to make eye-to-eye contact with an adult. They need to be trained in speaking clearly and distinctly so that other-than-family members can understand them. These graces will not come without practice. Have **"Pretend to Meet the Friend"** sessions where each child gets to be the friend and each child has a turn at being the child who looks at the adult and who speaks so he can be understood. The winners get to speak to humans outside of your home.

Privacy is an extremely important concern. Your child's right to privacy differs at each stage of his development but must be respected all along the line.

Your toddler learns the concept of privacy when you speak of it in terms of your own. Perhaps you want privacy in the bathroom or the bedroom. You emphasize the concept by closing your door and teaching the child to knock and wait for an answer before he barges in. While he is in his negative stage, he will demand some privacy from you. When his anger subsides, he will want to be with you. That is probably when you will want to have your privacy.

The next round of learned privacy will probably come when you start to spend "private time" with your child. Some families set aside a specific time of the day or the week for private time with each child. Some parents prefer to wait until the children clamor for attention all at once. Then they sort out the problem by giving private time for each on a rotating basis. However you allocate private time, your child will develop a warm feeling for it.

His room or his section of a shared room should be his private place. He may retreat there for complete privacy as long as he does not lock the door (this should be a rule in case of emergency) and he does not have dangerous items in his room. Just as you expect him to do, you must show courtesy by knocking on his door before opening it. If he does not want you to come in, don't. Just say that you are available for him when he feels ready.

As he reaches his teen years and wants to entertain in his room, you will have to decide together what the house rules will be about members of the same sex and those of the opposite.

When you are in his room, you still need to respect his privacy by not going into drawers that he has designated off limits. Certainly, diaries and notes are his and his alone. They were not meant for you and may not be read by you. Why does your teen have to be so secretive? He has to, because he is trying to grow apart from you and the family so that he will be able to be independent someday. If you are concerned during this hard period of pulling away from you that the ties of the family are not strong enough or that you would like to communicate better with him, try the **"Secret Note a Night."** You and he write a note to each other. It can be about anything. Neither note will be criticized or shared with anyone who is not in on the game. Whether you write about your activities or your feelings, it does not matter. What matters is that you are sharing with each other. Sometimes it is easier to write something down rather than to say it directly to one another. In any event, let these notes which are addressed to you be the only ones you read.

Nowadays, the telephone and computer are the most important links from your child to his friends. Just as you have trained your young child to allow you to have a few moments of privacy on the telephone, now your pre-teen and teen demand that same privacy. You have the right to limit the length of the phone calls or the time during which they may be made or received. However, who calls your child and whom your child calls and what is being said at either end are private.

Also, during his second decade, your child has a right to the privacy of his body. Is this teen, who covers up his body even when he is the only one in the room, the same one who used to run around naked at every opportunity? Yes, one and the same, but now that his body is developing sexually, he needs to have his privacy. When your son has a nocturnal emission, it should be treated as a normal part of his sexual development. He must be afforded his privacy. When your daughter begins to menstruate, the same is true. Take your cue from her. If she wants to be open about her periods or if she prefers that no living soul know about them, that is her prerogative. Abide by her wishes.

When a teen becomes more aware about his body, he may feel uncomfortable about visits to the doctor. This scenario is especially true with a daughter and a male doctor. It may be to your advantage to send her to a female doctor. In any event, you can explain that the doctor is a professional who looks at a person's body to examine it, not to gloat over it or laugh at it. Your child's concerns are real to her and should be discussed. Perhaps you can suggest that a favorite nurse be present or that you be in the examining room if that will make your child feel more comfortable.

For regular visits to the doctor, your child is entitled to take a list of written questions in with him. He should be quite relieved to know that the things he is experiencing happen to other children also. When any kind of medical procedure is to be done, the child has a right to know exactly what is supposed to happen. This is especially true when your daughter has an appointment with a gynecologist. She may feel afraid or embarrassed and not even know why. Tell her what will happen and how you feel during gynecological exams. She will be relieved to know that they are not your favorite ways to pass the time, either.

I went through a stage of wanting to see only women gynecologists. I figured they had experienced what I was going through and they would be more understanding. Some of them were, and some of them were not. My lesson was that a doctor needs to have a combination of technical knowledge, communication skills, and empathy. If he or she has these things, keep that gem. If not, look for a more well-rounded doctor who can establish a rapport with your child and with you. Remember, though, that doctors have the same shortcomings and strengths we all have.

Another major responsibility your child has is sharing. There are good things about living in a family, and there are bad things. Some children consider that sharing is a good thing. Others consider it one of the worst possible things to do. But by the very nature of being in a family, the child must share– his possessions, his time, and his feelings.

I found that sharing was difficult for me to teach and for my children to learn. It took me a long time to realize how important a possession was to a toddler. At that age, he thinks that what is his is part of him. It doesn't matter that he is surrounded by hundreds of toys. He will inevitably want the one that some other child wants at that moment. Also, why should he have to give up something just because a playmate wants it?

Alas, his social interaction should be, but isn't, on par with society's expectations. So you have to warn him that he may play with the toy for two more minutes. Then it will be given to his friend. By the same token, when he demands to have something his friend is using, you need to warn both participants of the two minutes left on the sharing meter. Sometimes, you need to take away a toy that they all want at the same time. Try to divert them to another project, but if they are at the grabbing stage, they will probably start to argue over the next toy, whatever it may be. If that is the case, you need to get them interested in something else.

Special things, like his favorite stuffed animal or his comfort blanket, are not up for sharing negotiation. They are his alone. Other things he feels are special may be kept in a separate location. Anyone who comes to play must be told that the toys on that certain shelf are not for sharing, but that everything else is.

When your child does hand over a toy to a playmate or does wait patiently to receive a toy, he deserves praise such as, "I like the way you shared" or "I like the way you waited for your turn." This constant positive reinforcement is the best way to keep him on his sharing toes. If you have been to a home or a playgroup where two other children have been having trouble sharing toys, perhaps when you leave there, you and your angel can discuss how the others could have shared better. Of course, since your child wasn't the guilty one this time, he will be overflowing with suggestions on how the others should have behaved. Remember some of his ideas for the next time he needs a refresher lecture on sharing.

An older child, who already is heavily into social interaction, usually doesn't have so much trouble sharing. But he too should be entitled to decide where he should keep his few prized possessions. At this stage, two other problems arise. These are which seat is his in the car and which shows will be watched on the television. If you are unwilling to buy a separate car and television for each child, then you will all have to realize that a plan like sharing-the-days is needed.

We play **"Whose Day Is It?"** There are variations like "Whose Week Is It?" or the game my husband and I like so much– "Whose Child Is That?" We have assigned the children different days of the week when they are the deciders about who sits where in the car and what television program can be watched during set hours. Of course, there can be negotiations, but that child is the dictator of the day. This plan works on several levels. First, it theoretically does away with the bickering over who gets to do what. Second, it gives each child a voice in making decisions on his own. Third, it takes the parents off the hook of having to decide who does what when. We notice that sometimes the children build up resentment and will retaliate when the time comes for them to be the decision-maker. But more often than not, they will enter into a give-and-take scenario with each other.

Other chores around the house can be assigned by **"Whose Day Is It?"** But when it is a chore rather than a privilege involved, you may have to keep your own record of who is responsible when. For some reason, they don't remember the chores as well as the privileges.

The sharing of their time is a responsibility easy to overlook in our fast-paced society. Children are accountable to themselves, their teachers, their friends, and their family. Family is the last on the list, because it is the one usually given the least amount of time. There are many demands made on everyone's schedule, but if you don't clear special time to spend together, you are not getting the most out of your life.

Some families designate Friday or Sunday dinner as the time for family, nuclear or extended. Lasting rituals can be started and passed on during these times. When your older children know about these scheduled occasions ahead of time, they take the responsibility to make their plans accordingly. However, remember that the dance or party or meeting they would rather attend may be important enough to them for you to excuse them once in a while.

You can enjoy the family tradition of a once-a-month talent show in your family. You "perform" something, whether it be your latest piece you have been practicing on your musical instrument or a song you learned in school or a crazy dance you just feel like doing. It is important to allow each member to have a turn in a non-competitive way.

Another productive way to share time with each other is to tell "**Round Robin Stories,**" already mentioned. Each person adds a word or a sentence or a paragraph to a story. This game is also great for car trips along with such old-time favorites as I Spy with my Little Eye, In Grandmother's Trunk, Geography, and anything having to do with license plates. Whatever you choose to do as a family, you need to try to involve all different age levels. Maybe you can bend rules for the younger ones and make the rules more challenging for the older folks.

The hardest responsibility for some children is to share inner feelings. Some thoughts should be kept to himself, because he may be trying to work out some private issues or hostile feelings. But, to prevent the scenario where your child and you feel that you really don't know him, you have to try to learn about him. What does he believe? What is important to him? What are his likes and dislikes, his fears and joys?

A younger child may tell you his thoughts constantly, but as he matures, he may keep them to himself or want to share them only with his friends. There is no guaranteed way to make him talk, but by your interest and your non-judgmental listening, you can open the lines of good communication. He can better share his feelings if he knows that you will listen openly. You should take these opportunities to share your feelings as well.

You can help a child work out some fears if you admit that many people have the same fear or that you were or are afraid of the same thing. When my seven-year-old learned that I used to be afraid of burglars when I was her age, she breathed a sigh of relief that she wasn't the only one who had this fear. She also felt that I was more human. We parents have to guard against putting ourselves up on an unrealistic pedestal. Soon enough, our teens will be chopping away at our pedestal, so we might as well try to give a realistic picture of ourselves all along the way. Yes, we can do some things well. Yes, we are failures at some things. Yes, when we were children, we misbehaved and had to be punished. Yes, we were afraid of many things. When you can feel comfortable opening up in friendly, sharing conversations with your child, he will feel better about opening up to you. The result will be a closer family bond.

The third category of children's responsibilities and rights pertains to those things he should do from his heart. These are things like giving gifts, doing good deeds, being honest, being praised, and being respected. As opposed to the duties he has to do with his hands and his minds, these are not necessities. They are the graceful and meaningful attributes which make for a complete individual.

A small child loves to give you things. Whether it be a piece of newspaper from your floor or a flower from your garden (or someone else's garden), he loves to see your reaction. You need to encourage him to continue to give tokens of his love for you. Later, when he can make scribbles on paper, treat each one with importance, hanging some on your special arts and crafts wall and taking some to your office.

When they are finally old enough to understand that others can have birthdays, they should be encouraged to make or help in the buying of an appropriate gift for someone else. At holidays and for special occasions, we take the children separately to the store to allow them to choose what they think is the perfect gift. Then they hide the selection under their bed or in a drawer until the big moment comes to present the gift. They need to know that just as they love to receive gifts, they can bestow on others that same special feeling by giving to them.

Gifts do not have to be expensive or even tangible, for that matter. Suggest to him the category of **"I Promise You"** gifts, which are slips of paper on which he writes a promise to do a certain chore or project for a week or a month. Or it can be that he promises to take you to your favorite movie or museum during this next month. Or maybe he will relieve you of one of your chores for a week. Often, these types of promise gifts are much more meaningful than a store-bought gift. Whatever the gift, he should have a say in its choice and a smile at its giving.

The next responsibility he has is that of doing good deeds. He must be taught that he can help himself be a better person by helping people. He can even start in his own home. Play **"See What I Can Do Today"** once a month. He looks around and finds something he can do that will help out the family. It has to be something that is apart from his chores. Sometimes play that he should do it and not tell anyone what he has done. Then the rest of you have to guess. Think of all that could be accomplished in your home if all the family members played.

After he understands the concept of doing good deeds, he can then enlarge his territory. He can do good deeds for those in the community. Some examples are helping to clean out the trash from vacant lots, calling a home-bound elderly person each day to say hello, playing his musical instrument in retirement or nursing homes, reading a story over the phone to a sick friend, caring for a neighbor's pet while she is away, or bringing in the newspaper each day to someone who needs help.

These are only a few examples of good deeds that a child can do. They are not done for pay. They are to be done out of the goodness of your child's heart. Donations to charity also fall into this group of good deeds. When you establish good habits of giving, you are building children who will make wonderful marks on society as they grow.

The next attribute you need to nurture is honesty. What degrees of honesty fit into your family? Do you cheat on your taxes? Do you fudge on your diet? When is a social lie acceptable? No one is totally honest all the time. But we need to strive to be honest in our actions and our feelings so that our relationships will be strong.

A child moves through different stages of lying. The four-year-old who exaggerates is just beginning to understand what is true and what is not. The school age child has to be taught that a teacher can usually see who is cheating on a test. (It is amazing how much a teacher can observe by standing in front of the room.) Cheating, lying, stealing, and all related negative behaviors are wrong and are usually discovered no matter how children try to cover up. A good technique to help your child develop aversions to these bad habits is the **"What's Wrong in This Story?"** game. Someone makes up a short tale involving a person who has lied or cheated or stolen. The others have to decide what the wrong thing the person did was and how he could rectify the situation. Of course, you can use as raw material for your stories scenes from real life in your home. Sometimes, these morals are learned better if the child feels a bit removed from the teaching. That way he doesn't have to be so defensive, and it is hoped that he will remember the lesson for the next time he is in a similar situation.

Every child has the right to be praised for his deeds. Praise for children is as important a life-nourishing substance as sunlight is for plants. We all need praise to feel loved and wanted. The warmth from the praise envelops us in a cloak of emotional well-being, which makes our lives fuller and richer. Of course you love your child, but if you don't tell him or don't give him the demonstrable love that praise offers, he may not understand the message you are intending to convey. Have your praise to him be honest. Even after a very trying day, you can certainly think of something positive to say. Maybe it is only that he brushed his teeth carefully that evening. But at least it is better to reinforce the positive than to dwell on the negative.

Every child also has a right to be respected. He should be respected not because he received a good grade on a project or because he was the first one to be toilet trained on your block. He is to be respected because he is a person, an individual. He needs to know that you will love him forever, no matter what. He needs to know that you will be on his side as long as he follows the rules of your family and of society. He needs to know that you respect him enough to trust him. He needs to be able to come to you with any problem and know that the two of you will try to solve it. He needs to know that you are on his side, that you will do all you can to provide a warm, loving, respecting environment for him.

My father lives by the concept that the greatest gift a father can give to his children is to love their mother. Taken a few steps further, as we did in my home, the greatest gifts you can all give yourselves is to love each other. The rights and responsibilities of children are necessary for them to coexist in a family. They are the means by which a child can make use of his hands, mind, and heart so that he will become a well-rounded, loving member of your family.

PRODUCTION:
SIBLING RIVALRY

Chapter Ten:
Sibling Rivalry

Chapter Ten: Sibling Rivalry

Sibling rivalry will exist no matter what you do, unless you have just one child. As soon as you have a second child, you have all the actors in place for a production of "Sibling Rivalry" starring your children. Whether your production will be a major or a minor one is, in part, determined by how you handle their feelings. All children want to be the most loved and the most important in your eyes.

You will need to assure them over and over that your eyes are capable of seeing more than one person at a time, that your arms can give as many hugs as people want, and that there will always be enough room on your lap for all your children.

You would need reassurance too if your spouse one day announced that because she or he loved you so much, she or he was going to bring home another adult to live with you. You would need some time to get used to this unusual situation, and you probably would never learn to like the "intruder."

Children can feel unwanted with the arrival of another cute actor. Your task as director of this minor showing of our play is to provide each child with reassurance in words and deeds. However, the time may come when you feel that you can't possibly spend enough time with each child. You are exhausted to begin with, so how can you possibly deal with all the demands on you?

Follow the simple "age" rule– the youngest gets most of your time simply because he needs more done for him. The next oldest gets the next amount of time, and so on, until the oldest person in the house, adults included, gets the smallest amount of time, but certainly the deepest quality time. Keep in mind that since you are part of the family, you need time for yourself too.

Once you have decided that each person needs different amounts of your time, how do you know when to give time to whom? The baby will tell you in no uncertain terms when it is his turn. A slightly older child will demand the time, but he will have to accept the fact that you will be with him in five minutes or when the kitchen timer rings or when the baths are over. His sibling rivalry becomes inflamed when he thinks you are spending too much time with the other children. So you need to emphasize to him that different jobs take different amounts of time, and that when you have time for him, you will be able to work on his favorite project with him. The time may not be exactly even, but it will certainly be spent with love and enjoyment.

You can also play **"Mommy/Daddy Helpers"** with your older children who are over two. Tell them that sometimes you have more work than you can possibly do yourself. Would they please be your helpers? You can even have a formal induction ceremony, complete with badges designating them as your helpers. Then whenever you feel it is necessary, ask them to help you with some job. Perhaps they can reach a diaper or sort the socks or put all the blocks on the left side of the room (certainly not away where they belong!). By focusing their energies, you are making them feel like partners instead of outsiders who need to throw imaginary rocks at you to be noticed.

The point is you do have a great deal to do, but you also have several people for whom you are responsible. The more often you can have them play on your team rather than their being part of the opposition, so much the better and so much the less rivalry with which you will have to contend at any given moment.

Further honest explanations to your children will help them

understand some of their feelings. "I am frustrated that I can't spend as much time with you as I did before the baby came. Can you help me solve my problem?" Don't be surprised if he says that he understands that the baby takes up much of your time, and that he will be happy if you can play two games a day with him. Children's reasoning powers blossom when nurtured with honesty and respect.

Another pressure you may feel is that you can never get anything done. Perhaps your older child needs new shoes, and the baby's birth announcements haven't been addressed in the last eight weeks. The only time that passes slowly is the nine months of a second pregnancy. Once the baby is here, the hours speed by, and you can't get anything accomplished.

Now that we have discussed some major worries you may have because of the birth of a second or third child or more, we can turn our attention to something with which your children are becoming acquainted, the ugly monster of sibling rivalry. How can we contain this monster, knowing that he will never go away completely? How can we tame him? He will live in your house as an uninvited guest, but you are determined to allow him only a minor part in your life drama.

The monster is certainly green, green for jealousy. Let's label him aloud, so your children realize that this feeling they have is jealousy and is a normal feeling. A three-year-old needs the assurance that you can love more than one person completely. An eight-year-old has to be shown that even though he may not be as cute as the smaller children, like a kitten who has grown into a cat, he can be loved and appreciated for the things he can do as a cat. They all must be encouraged to express their feelings of jealousy, but their actions must be acceptable. Hitting a sibling is not allowed. Since a pre-schooler could possibly injure a baby seriously, don't leave the two alone until you can trust the older one. Using a punching bag or smashing a "designated hitter" doll or punch pillow while he yells that he is angry about the sibling are all acceptable expressions of how he feels. "You don't have to like your sister today, but you cannot hurt her." I also recommend punching pillows for parents to use when they need to express their anger. Urge the children in releasing their anger to "use words, not hands."

Many angry and jealous feelings can be released during role playing and psycho-drama as you play **"Bickering Brains."** Choose one of the hundred bickering conversations you heard all day, and have each child play the other one in that situation. Interesting points will be brought up during these sessions. Have each child summarize what he learned from being in someone else's shoes.

Tell them how jealous you used to feel about your siblings. They probably won't believe you, but by stirring up old feelings, you may be more compassionate about the stages in which your children are now struggling.

Rivalry manifests itself differently at different stages and with different age spreads. Experts currently suggest that the optimal spacing between children is three years. By the time your first child is about three, he is no longer so dependent upon you. His world has enlarged enough to include his nursery school, his other playmates, and his important scientific experimentation. Indeed, this is about the time when many parents feel that they are not needed so much any more and may decide to have another child.

However, no matter how you have spaced your children, and often you don't have so much control over when they are actually conceived, you are bound to witness some sibling rivalry. Whether it is between the first and second or the first and last born or whatever your combinations are, when you see the ugly green monster rear its head, acknowledge its presence. It may be disguised as the oldest child correcting or criticizing the sibling who threatens his throne in the family. Or it may be the unhappy baby of the family annoying the taller members.

The cure for "middle child syndrome" is simple. Whenever you feel that your middle child is lashing out—either blatantly or covertly—because he is a middle child, call in all the actors for a cast meeting. Play **"Plus and Minus."** Each one of your actors should tell an advantage and a disadvantage about his placement in the family. The oldest one can stay up later but has more chores during the day.

The baby gets more cuddling attention but can't participate in the evening activities. The parents can do what they want when they want to but have to care for a sick child in the middle of the night. By this time, the middle child's complaints pale in comparison to the troubles everyone else has expressed. Once he has heard in open communication how the others feel they are being treated, he will be able to view his placement in the family with a little more objectivity. The creed you may express often can be "There are good points and bad points to your placement (or your age), but they are all part of being in a family."

As much as you can, ignore their arguments. They often bicker just enough to have you step in and blame one or the other. If you do this, you are giving negative or positive reinforcement, and chances are great that you will never really know who started it. That fact is not even important now. The behavior has to stop, no matter who is guilty and who is innocent. "I don't want to know anything now about it except that it will stop." When someone settles down, "I like the way so-and-so is behaving." You are only rewarding by giving attention to positive behavior. "You played so nicely together that I am going to give you special hugs." Or you can use a sibling behavior chart where a child gets a star on the chart when he has shown good sibling behavior or demonstrated some good feeling toward a sibling for any period of time. If your children have not gotten along together for years, you may want to reward them for ten minutes of acceptable togetherness. You can work your way up to hours and then days of getting along better when you reward positive behavior. Never compare them on the chart to each other. Only compare them to themselves, that is, how they are behaving better now as opposed to how they used to behave.

You should know when to change the scenery in the rivalry drama. Sometimes, you'll need to put the children in the car and go for a drive. At other times, you'll have to send them outside to play or to run around the house five times. After they burn off some excess energy, they may be more human. Also, planned roughhousing where wrestling, tickling, and rolling around are allowed as long as no one hurts the other is a social outlet for aggression.

If a certain object is the cause of an argument, simply remove it or turn it off or unplug it saying, "You may have this back when you can use it properly." In other words, you have to decide when to ignore the results of the rivalry, when to interfere, when to change scenery, and when to change tactics. Each situation demands a different reaction or non-reaction on your part, so it is almost impossible to react consistently. Follow your best instincts. If something isn't working, change it. If it works, great.

Some other suggestions for living with sibling rivalry revolve around games. Play **"Solve Someone Else's Problem"** by sitting in a circle with the children. Make up other children's names and ages, and explain their misbehaviors. Have each child give his suggestions for helping "that" person solve his problem. Of course, you have poetic license to submit your own family's problems for discussion.

Play **"My Appreciation Day."** The child who needs some extra attention is the object of his own appreciation day wherein people tell him wonderful things about himself and on which he is allowed to decide what food will be served. In fact, people of all ages should have appreciation days. They work wonders for moods and attitudes.

Play **"Rainy Day Transformation"** on days when, for reasons of weather or other factors, your plans have been changed. Don't resent the fact that you have to be with them all day. Refocus. View the day as a gift enabling you to do something special with the children. Do something (yes, it can be for a short amount of time) terrific with each child and then a group activity which pleases most of you. Keep your attitude upbeat, and the mood will be catching. During the sunshine days, add ideas to your rainy day box, so you will be prepared for a blizzard of time together.

Play **"You Are Our Guest."** Each sibling should be encouraged to treat the others as though they were guests in your home. Say, "Would you really yell about that to a guest?" "How would you share that with a guest?" Because each child will much prefer being the guest himself, this concept may help you explain getting along together to all of them.

Play **"But Do You Remember When You Were a Baby?"** This

works especially well when your older child is feeling overwhelmed by jealousy toward a baby. Reassure him that when he was a baby he was that cute, that cuddly, and that gorgeous. Show him pictures of how he looked, and play his baby videos and tape recordings. Tell him what skills he now has about which you are proud.

As parents of siblings, you have to resign yourself to the fact that the rivalry they feel is normal. If they didn't argue, bicker, and act obnoxious to each other at least some of the time or even much of the time, they probably wouldn't be mentally healthy children. Bless them for being normal, and go into another room to scream when your frustration level gets too high. You then will feel much better and be able to face the next round of rivalry revelry. Children's tolerance levels are higher than ours; what bothers us maybe won't bother them for many more minutes. So the more garbage from them you ignore and the more you let them solve the problems themselves, the better for you and the more growth experiences possible for them. Look at the bright side. Even when they plot together against the parents, at least they are working together with each other.

Eventually, they will outgrow the blatant rivalry, and you will realize that your children really did listen to your explanations of how humans should behave. They will more than likely have their siblings as friends for their adulthood in spite of their moaning to the contrary in their childhood. Your best strategy to keep your sibling rivalry drama off-off Broadway and to live with each other for the next couple of decades is to supply them with an infinite number of hugs, personal doses of self-esteem, positive reinforcement, and a great deal of happy time together.

ROMANCE

Chapter Eleven: Parental Roles

Chapter Eleven: Parental Roles

You met. You dated. You fell in love. You married. You spent idyllic times together as a couple. Now all of that is ruined. You are parents. And your frustration and exhaustion levels often prevent you from enjoying each other. Sometimes your misplaced emotions alienate you from the one who is the dearest to you.

What is the solution to this problem? Pleasant parenting. The first rule to remember is that your spouse is your best friend, not your enemy. You need to treat him or her as you would a friend in your home. You are both members of a team working for the same goal of raising a happy, loving family. Yes, you can disagree with each other. Yes, you can argue. Yes, you can do these things in front of the children.

You need to be free and honest with your emotions. If something bothers you, tell your spouse. If you can communicate in an open manner, you can remain friends with your lover. State your problem in I-messages as described by Dr. Thomas Gordon in his *Parent Effectiveness Training*. Say things like "I feel ignored when you read the paper when I want to share my day with you" instead of "you are lazy and don't care about me." Or "I feel overwhelmed with my mothering job today, and I need a break for a few hours" instead of "you are an uncaring father and husband." Name-calling and labeling make the other person defensive and more likely to retaliate.

Experts recommend that the person who is listening restate what the first one has said to make certain he has understood it. Also, when you are fighting, don't bring up past hurts. Stick to the problem at hand. Make sure both sides agree to and understand the solution. Play **"I Prefer to Make Up"** after arguments, because the making-up can be a good time to express how you really feel about each other.

Much of the frustration stems from the fact that being a parent is an enormous task. Even on the best of days, your child may have mood swings that grate on your nerves. Whether you are a househusband, or a full-time working-outside-of-the-house wife, or the more traditional parents, you have to juggle time, emotions, and tasks all day long. You need to remember that you are both in this operation together. You are partners and must share as much of the parenting load as possible. This sharing is the best way to prevent parent burnout.

Many parents of newborns do so correctly from the start. If the mother is nursing, the father can do some of the other chores like bathing the baby or changing the diapers. Some fathers give the 11:00 p.m. bottle of formula or expressed milk, which enables the exhausted mother to retire early. Whatever task the father chooses to do, he will soon come to enjoy the bonding and the feeling that he is needed. So often, the father of a newborn feels left out because the mother is the primary care giver. But he can make himself useful and feel more of a partner in this lifetime endeavor.

Another solvable problem is the twenty-four hour syndrome. When the mother is the primary at-home parent, she is really working day and night. No matter how much you like any job, you can't do it twenty-four hours a day without a break from the physical and psychological demands. The mother needs something she can do that is just for herself. Some women decide to work full-time, some part-time. Some take a class like exercise or calligraphy. Whatever it is, it must be something where you can think for two minutes without having someone short interrupt you.

Another suggestion which would give further relief to the primary care giver is to play **"Rotating Days."** On the weekends, the husband is entitled to sleep late. But so is the wife. In our home, we rotated weekend days. I would wake up with the children early on Saturdays, and my husband would on Sundays. The same system worked well on our vacations. If the mother has to administer the same childcare on vacations as she does all the other days, then what is the point of being on a vacation? No matter what the length of our vacation, we would alternate days. The first day would be my husband's. He would be responsible for arising early, playing with, feeding, and diverting the children. I had the entire day free from parental responsibility, even though I was right next to them. Sometimes, I would have a hard time controlling my joy at feeling free. But, sometimes, I would volunteer to help with the tasks. Knowing that I didn't have to was a great relaxer. The next day my husband would be "off," and it would be my day. By using this system, we traveled the country and the world with the children, feeling that we really were on vacation.

As parents, you two are entitled to private time with each other. I feel strongly that you should have babysitters from the beginning. Parents argue that they could never leave their babies because they are so small or because they would cry. The response to those concerns is that you will leave him with a qualified person and he will probably cry if you stay home anyway. Many babies have a built-in radar that makes them cry when a sitter enters your home and makes them stop when you close your front door as you leave. They cry just enough to make you feel guilty. Then they usually stop and have a perfectly delightful time.

Whatever happens in the house when you are gone, as long as it is safe, should not worry you. When you are out of the house, you should concentrate on developing your couple potential, just as your baby should be allowed to develop his potential to handle himself with those other than you.

There are many ways to choose a babysitter. I have known parents who allow only women over sixty to babysit. I personally prefer the less strict approach of employing twelve- or thirteen-year-olds because they are in the responsible years before dating, and they are available more often. Whether you use relatives, teenagers, retired persons, or agency sitters, you have the responsibility to explain what you expect from them while you are gone. Give them a tour of each room of your house. Show them how you want them to exit in case of a fire. Point out your smoke alarms, extinguishers, flashlights, candles, etc. Leave the pertinent phone numbers in a conspicuous location, and try to return home close to the time you promised. This time is the stage of life when you may suddenly find yourself with a curfew again, because your sitter can't be out after a certain hour.

If you take your child to a sitter's home while you work or recreate, you have the right to check whether that house meets adequate safety standards.

A child goes through stages of being sitter-friendly and sitter-afraid. As long as you and the sitter understand that these are stages, you will feel much better. It helps to explain to your child that you will be going out, that the sitter will come at a certain time, that he can play games and have snacks with her, and that she will put him to sleep. Assure him that when you come home, you will peek on him and give him a big kiss. When he knows what to expect, he can handle the transition more easily. You can explain that he has special outings with Mommy and with Daddy and that now this outing is special just for the adults.

When you will be gone for several days, you should leave a full schedule for the sitter. After you have written out almost hour-by-hour what needs to be done with the young children, you will be amazed that you yourself actually accomplish all that. It will be at that point that you will know that you deserve the planned trip.

The importance of making time for you two adults to spend together cannot be overstated. When you become parents, you face a definite shift in your relationship. Instead of spending time gazing lovingly into each other's eyes, you now find that you enjoy watching your partner smile lovingly into the eyes of your child.

No matter how tired you both are or how involved in other projects you become, you must make time for each other. Some couples like to schedule a specific time for a rendezvous. Others like the idea of spontaneity. Use whichever method best suits your lifestyle and moods.

If the two of you have trouble deciding when to make love, keep in mind what sex educators have discovered. Women have different monthly hormonal levels which help dictate their moods, and men are often aroused faster than women. So if one of you is in the mood and the other one is not, try starting with some romantic groundwork. Play **"How Romantic Can I Get?"** See which spouse can do the more romantic thing. The old stand-bys of flowers and candy really work. And there is no rule that prohibits the wife from showering the husband with these treats. Also, you can have a special dessert by candlelight after the children are asleep. A change of mood can work wonders. Remember that if the wife has been mothering all day in the house, that amount of time is the equivalent to the husband working overtime at the office. She could use some change of routine, and what better than to share romance and loving with her spouse?

In addition to igniting the flames of romance and sex as often as you both like, you need to speak about your love relationship frequently. Even though it is understood between you that you love each other, you still need to say it aloud over and over. Play **"What I Love About You"** by discussing the five most wonderful qualities your spouse possesses. Tell him or her why he or she is such a good mate and parent. Describe what you would say to your loved ones if you knew you had two more minutes to live. Create special love holidays that are significant for the two of you. My husband and I celebrate our wedding anniversary monthly with special time and special words for each other. If you don't make time for each other, before you know it, the time has slipped away.

Children learn from example. You certainly want them to develop into warm, loving adults. So of course it is all right for you and your spouse to kiss and hug and hold hands in front of the young children. Depending on how comfortable you are with your body, you can undress and use the bathroom in front of the children. They need to continue their sex education, which begins at their birth. Whenever you stroke their beautiful bodies, bathe, and change them, you are helping them appreciate that their bodies can give them pleasure. As they develop and begin to masturbate, you need to reinforce the idea that what they do to their bodies feels pleasurable but that they need to do it in private. Let them know what rooms you consider private, perhaps their rooms, perhaps some other place at home. You can also reinforce the idea that Mommy and Daddy are entitled to privacy. When your bedroom door is closed, the children must knock before entering. You must extend the same courtesy to them. Always knock before you enter their room.

When the time comes for the "birds and bees" lecture, you need to be prepared. The library has many sex education books written at all levels. Read them ahead of time. Always give factual answers. Give proper names to the parts of the body. If you treat the discussion of sex honestly, you teach your child to be honest about it.

The rites of passage, which include the question of how babies are made, the developing body, the beginning of menstruation, the first bra, the first shaving experience, and the beginning of dating, are happy and sad at the same time. Parents are ambivalent about wanting their children to grow up.

Inevitably, the milestones appear. In the beginning, they are when you put away the crib and diapers. Then comes the time when you smile at each other because you realize that you have been allowed to sleep late on the weekends. Then come the school years. Step by step, the children grow away from us, as they should. Finally, the day will come when there are just the two of you at home together. If you have been strengthening your bonds as a couple all these years, you should be well-equipped to face the future together.

GRAND)TIME

Chapter Twelve:
The Grandparents—
or the Grand Parents

Chapter Twelve:
The Grandparents—
or the Grand Parents

When you gave birth to a child you probably didn't realize it then, but you also gave birth to as many as four grandparents at the same time. No wonder the birthing experience was so draining! You created a child, and you created grandparents at the same time.

If, for any reason, you do not have actual grandparents for your child, you should find people who will substitute in that role. Whether you choose to "adopt" an elderly neighbor or an older friend or someone from a nearby retirement home, you will be enriching the lives of that adopted person, of your child, and of yourself. Grandparents, whether actual or adopted, add a new perspective to your family unit. They serve as a reminder of the continuity of life, the passing of generations, and of what the world used to be like. You need the give and take inherent in this kind of relationship. You need to see the pleasure on the faces of the youngest and the oldest in your enlarged family unit. You need grandparents for your child, and the grandparents need you and your family.

This scenario sounds fine, you may be thinking, for those parents who get along with their own parents. But what about the rest of us who, for whatever reasons, cannot tolerate being with our parents? What if we never had a normal relationship with them before? How can we start now? How can we ever erase the bad memories?

There are two major reasons for a bad relationship between adults and their parents. The first one is that either you or your parents feel that one of you did something or some things terrible to the other. Unless the wrongness was something criminal or immoral, you will be much better off if you can swallow your pride or whatever else is at stake and clear the air. Whether you have to apologize or sit down and have a heart-to-heart airing with each other, do it. Play the **"Let's Put the Past Behind Us"** game. Say, "I feel that having a grandparent relationship for my child is important for him and for you. Whatever happened in the past, we need to put behind us. Let's start from this moment to build a three generational family. I need your help."

If this approach doesn't work, try again when your child is older. If, after you have tried your best and it still doesn't work out, cultivate a substitute grandparent, but still leave open the lines of communication between the two of you.

The second reason for a bad relationship is that you have not developed a strong enough image of yourself as a capable adult. If this is the case, you need to grow up. Define what the problem is and work on strengthening the part or parts of you that are weak. If you feel your parent walks all over you, move out of the way figuratively. If you feel your parents still think of you as a child, play the **"Guess What I Am Capable of Now"** game. Say, "Mom and Dad, I am at an interesting point in my life. I have finished my schooling. I am married. I have set up housekeeping. And I am also a parent. I am feeling very much an adult. I have thought about how you were as parents and have decided that I want to use your methods of blank, blank, and blank. I also want to redefine my relationship with you as one of adult to adult. I look forward to valuing your companionship on this level."

Of course, both you and your adult parent will have to believe what you said. If a confrontation arises where you feel that you are not being treated as the adult you are, tell your parent exactly what bothers you. Be specific. Don't throw the entire list of sins of the human race at him or her. Work on one problem at a time. Believe that you are able to stand on your own two feet. No matter how sour things have turned between the two or three of you in the past, it is worth the effort to try to sweeten the present.

What if there are recurring problems with your older parents? Let's say your parent says something to make you feel guilty about your parenting like "Why don't you put a heavier jacket on the baby?" Now your usual pattern was that you would a) say something like "stop mixing in" and feel annoyed that you are not being treated as an adult, or b) put a heavier jacket on the baby and feel guilty that you aren't being as good a parent as you should.

In a case like this, you have to remember that both you and your parent have rights. He or she has the right to express his opinion about the jacket, although you have to train him or her to talk in a non-judgmental manner. You have the right to dress your child any way you deem fit. Therefore, you acknowledge his concern and then assert yourself in an equally non-judgmental way. "Thank you for being so concerned about the baby. But this is the jacket I have chosen for him to wear. I feel he'll be comfortable in it, but if I see that he is not, then I will put on a heavier one." Or if you are not as confident about your parenting modes yet, just say that your doctor (or your parenting teacher) feels that this weight jacket allows the baby's skin to perspire better. Sometimes you need to stretch the truth to stand up for yourself.

Perhaps you can cite numerous examples of what you feel is interference from your parents. If you treat their suggestions as their legitimate right to express themselves and your ideas as legitimate opinions you are entitled to hold, you will be seeing a healthier relationship between you.

Look at your usual patterns of disagreement. Then the next time something is about to happen that will upset you in the course of the recurring pattern, do one of three things. Go with it, avoid the situation, or change the pattern completely. Using the example of a mother who calls you every day, let's say that you feel she is checking up on you and you are bothered by her calls. You can continue with the pattern, that is, go with it, because you realize that she has a need to keep in touch. Or you can avoid the situation by not being home when she usually calls or by telling her at the beginning of the call that you don't have time to speak now. A more challenging choice is to play **"Change the Pattern Completely."** Be honest in your explanation. Say, "Mom, I know you want to keep in touch with what is happening here, but I feel uncomfortable that you call so often. I feel that you are checking up on me and that I am not independent enough. At this time, I feel I need to control my life a little more, so could you please do me a favor? Allow me to call you every few days for the next month. I will be happy to fill you in on our activities and hear what you have been doing. And I will feel a little more independent and a little more confident as a mother (or father)."

Try this change of pattern to see if you both can live with it. If one of you can't, then put your heads together to think up another solution to be tried. Keep presenting the problem in terms that it is your problem, that you need the other's help in solving it, and that if one solution doesn't work, you will think of another one. You both "save face" and possibly save a relationship in the process.

You grew up with the desire to become independent, but a time will come when you will want to become independent on an equal basis with your older parent. Try a give and take relationship. Play **"I'm Good at This, and You are Good at That."** You help each other according to your strong points. Maybe your optimism can help your parent through a hard part of an illness. Maybe your parents' experience can show you a better way to finish a project. By having this attitude, you can view your parents as assets, and you enrich all of your lives.

Now that I have suggested how to solve the problem of those of you with less than good relationships with your parents, we can concentrate on exactly what a happy, healthy, growing grandparent relationship should be. Your goal is to have everyone enjoy being together. You should feel fortunate to have three generations. You should elevate the grandparents to the level of Grand Parents.

Your children's grandparents either live close to you, or they don't. They may want to be participatory grandparents, or they may not. Whatever the situation really is, you have to find out what amount of grandparenting makes both of you feel comfortable. You do this by asking them and by evaluating what has happened after you have been together. They may be the kind of people who are still busy in their own lives and would rather not be babysitters. Or they may have been counting the days until all of you reached the point where they can be called upon to help with the grandchild. Or maybe they don't even know how they feel until they have been grandparents for a while.

You are entitled to set rules when they are in your home. They are entitled to set rules when you are in their home. If any of you is uncomfortable with a rule, discuss it with those involved. Don't let the feeling fester inside. That will only build resentment. You want to clear the air or reach a compromise or at least get the feelings out so you will feel better.

If the grandparents live far away so that your primary contact is by phone, you have the pleasure of deciding what will be the grandparent story to share during that phone call. They will love to share that special story with their friends over and over until they have another story about their precious family. You can play **"Capture the Memory"** by making a list of the grandparent stories. Many years later, you will enjoy reading over the list and remembering the antics of the children.

When these long-distance relatives do come to visit, or when you go to visit them, you will be able to enjoy a compressed, intense live-in together during which they will be able to enjoy being with the children. Now since children are children, they will behave like children during these visits. By this, I mean they will have their good moments and their bad hours. They will make you feel proud, and they will embarrass you. Probably, nothing you had planned will turn out exactly as you wanted, and someone will certainly get sick.

You adults need to keep your sense of humor. Laugh about the times when you were a child and behaved in some childish way. Explain to your parents that your children are at specific stages like grabbing or trying to shock the world with their vocabulary. I always tried to paint a murkier picture than what would really happen. This way, we would all be happily surprised at the end of the visits.

We each have selective memories, and grandparents are no exception. They generally remember what good children we were when we were young (which gives me hope that as time passes, I will block out the horrible times). So I suggest that you play **"How Bad Children Really Can Be"** in preparation for any lengthy visit by the grandparents. You tell them what mischief this age child can do. Explain the normal developmental stages in your home. Be sure to tell what unbelievably obnoxious thing another child did. Then your child will shine in comparison. You need to lower the expectation of your folks, so they will have a more realistic idea about the children.

For those of you with parents who live geographically close and can visit much more frequently, you need to examine the wants and needs of all of you. How often should you be in the other's home? What are the hours of visitation? What discipline methods will be allowed? How should criticism be handled? How should violations of rules be handled? I suggest you sit down and play **"Board Room Rules"** with your adult parents. Appoint the oldest member the chairperson of the board for this meeting. The next oldest is the recording secretary. Make a list of the concerns you have and the questions you need answered. Let each Board member have a say about each concern. Compromise, dictate, don't insult. Come to an agreement on all the rules that work best for your family dynamic. Write down the conclusions. Give each member a copy. Agree to meet again whenever anyone feels it is necessary. This formalized meeting will allow you to air your concerns so no member of the family will feel slighted or put-upon.

Grandparents need to keep in mind that parenting styles evolve slowly or change radically every few years. Maybe they were told the pacifier was the wrong thing to use, but now you feel that it is necessary. Just tell them that you are trying to be the best parent for their grandchild and that at this time you feel it is important to use the pacifier. They need to be able to express their opinion, and you need to express yours. But you have the final say, and you should be firm in your convictions until you feel you have to try something else. There is nothing wrong with admitting that you were wrong about something. You will be growing as a parent, just as you have grown at different stages.

Life as grandparents may be much easier if your parents follow these rules:

RULES FOR GRANDPARENTS

1. Give complete support to your children.

2. Let your children make their own mistakes. They do not have your experience or your knowledge, but they need to develop these on their own.

3. When you need to disregard rule number 2, express your opinions and disagreements in a non- judgmental way. "I feel that the baby needs to wear long pants" instead of "You are going to make that baby sick from the cold." You can be honest in your opinions but you can be honest in a cheerful manner.

4. Brag about your grandchildren *and* what wonderful parents your children are. But you also have to listen diligently to your friends when they brag about their families.

5. Remember that the times and the parenting styles may have changed since you were new parents. Some of the change is for the better. Some is not. But your children are adults and are doing their best. Try to see the positive side to what they are doing.

6. Don't ever put your grandchild in the position of having to mediate between you and your adult child.

7. Treat your grandchild as a unique individual. Don't compare his abilities or lack of them to others', especially to those of his parents or siblings.

8. Participate in Family Board Meetings openly and honestly. They are a specifically structured way for differences of opinion to be aired.

9. Tell your children how you feel about babysitting. If you do not want to do it, don't. If you do, establish the rules you will both follow.

10. Discuss and accept methods of discipline for your grandchildren, then follow them.

11. Periodically check to see if what you think are appropriate gifts really are. Ask if they would prefer a check or a gift. Some people have a strong opinion one way or the other. Even though you are afraid that what you choose will be the wrong size or not liked at all, the fact that you made the effort to choose something may be more important than the gift itself.

12. Be a careful observer. When your children are with the grandchildren, see how they calm them down. Learn the songs they sing together, even the hand motions. Or play **"Teach Grandma and Grandpa Something New."** Have your grandchild be the teacher, and you learn and practice a song or dance or game he teaches you.

13. Discuss with your children what both of you feel is the correct number of phone calls a day or a week or a month. Reach a compromise when necessary. Teach your grandchild your phone number as soon as he can learn it. You may be surprised when you pick up the receiver one day.

14. Read or tell a story to your grandchild almost every time you see him. Your actions will speak volumes.

15. Learn how to phrase a question so that the child will have to answer it in multi-syllabic sentences. Don't ask "How is school?" or "What did you do yesterday?" Instead, ask "What problems are you working on in math?" or "Tell me two places you went after lunch yesterday."

16. Share your past. Give tours of your photo albums and the treasured decorations in your home.

17. Babyproof your home when the grandchildren come for a visit. It isn't fair to them for you to leave your breakables and cleaning solutions and matchbooks where they can reach them. Be sure to cover your electrical outlets with safety caps while the children are very young.

18. Depending on the ages of the grandchild, you must expect when you get together with them: noise, spills, running noses, occasional vomit on your good clothing, loud unintelligible music, constant phone ringing, grabbing, rough-housing, odors, tantrums, and crying by any age member of the household. These are actions and activities that are part of a normal, mentally healthy family. Change your expectations, and enjoy the give and take around you.

19. Keep or develop your sense of humor.

20. Have private time with each grandchild separately. Cultivate an ongoing routine with each one. For example, you can test them on the capital cities of the world or the first names of the classical composers or the box scores in baseball. Establish special rituals for the two of you. You can even keep some of them from the rest of the family to make them even more special.

21. Keep your medical problems in proportion. Be honest about them, but remember that to others there are more important things in the world than how you feel that day.

22. Think more about the joy your grandchildren give you. If you are far away from them geographically or emotionally, start a letter writing campaign to your adult children and your grandchildren. As you establish a paper or email relationship, it will be more rewarding than having nothing at all. Consider exchanging video or cassette tapes if extended telephone calls are beyond your means.

23. Look into programs geared to grandparents and grandchildren. Some libraries have grandparent packs, which include books and games for you to play together. Some travel agencies plan trips for grandparents and their grandchildren. One tour operator is Grandtravel in Washington, DC. Another travel agency is Your Cruise Concierge in Bethesda, Maryland, which can arrange multi-generational cruise reunions for the whole family. When you do things together, with a good insight into the limitations of each age, you build sterling memories.

The constant themes running throughout a healthy parent-grandparent relationship are honesty, compromise, flexibility, and communication, with the escape valve of the Board Meeting. But as the elder parents age, new problems have to be addressed.

Although each person ages in a slightly different manner and has different medical and emotional concerns, many of the problems stem from the fact that the older adults are no longer able to meet your standards of honesty, compromise, flexibility, or communication. When your parents reach this stage, whether because of unchanneled retirement, illness, death of a spouse, depression, or the normal aging process, you have entered what has been called the sandwich generation. You are sandwiched between the needs of your children and the needs of your parents.

There is no doubt that the added burdens will be hard on you. But whether you view this period as a dainty finger sandwich or a massive submarine sandwich is completely in your control. There are steps you can take to ease your current load.

WAYS TO INTERACT WITH YOUR AGING PARENTS

1. Keep your sense of humor, and encourage your older parent to keep his or hers. A shared smile or laugh will go a long way in maintaining your mutual support.

2. Study the aging process, so that when your parent shows signs of confusion, you can assure him or her that what he or she is experiencing is something that is common, albeit upsetting for that age group. It is comforting to realize that some changes in behavior aren't so frightening when we know that they are expected.

3. Literally take them, if that is the only way they will go, to the doctor or doctors for a complete physical exam. There seem to be two groups of seniors– those who will not go to a doctor, no matter what, and those who make a second career of going to doctors whether or not the visits are justified. Many of their problems can be treated or their fears about imagined problems can be assuaged when the results of the tests are shared with them. I suggest you visit doctors

who give complete explanations of the test results. Take notes so there will be no forgetting.

4. Understand that routine becomes more and more important for your seniors. However, you should ncourage branching out if, for example, you observe that they are having the same lunch every day.

5. Respect them. No matter how feeble or forgetful or unhappy they become, you must tell them that you respect them. Both of you can lament the fact that aging can be very upsetting. You will be there soon enough and will want to have a sympathetic ear and still retain a large measure of your dignity.

6. Reassure them of your love for them. Talk often about your shared memories. Play **"Decide on a Decade."** One of you chooses a decade, and both of you tell what you remember from that time. What were the clothing styles? What did the family do together? Which relatives were in disfavor? What were the low points of that time period? What were the highlights? What world events affected the family? What music did you like then?

7. Teach your children, by example, to accept their grandparents' aging. The look of an elderly person or the sight of a wheelchair or the concept of death can all be very frightening to your child (not to mention to you and your aging parent). Answer the children's questions as honestly as you can. "No, I don't think Grandma will die while we are visiting her, but I can't be sure." "Grandpa is in a wheelchair, because his legs aren't strong enough to hold up his body anymore." "Grandma can't hear you unless you stand in front of her and speak clearly." "When people get old, their bodies slow down, but they can still have wonderful ideas in their minds and much love in their heart."

8. Encourage your parent to tell stories to your children. Record vignettes of his story, and transcribe the tapes. Ask questions chronologically, thematically, and then philosophically. One memory will trigger another, and, if your parent can no longer remember, then find another relative who can fill in the missing blanks. A family history does wonders in bringing you closer together with your aging

parent. If you prefer, you can hire a professional oral historian to record the stories.

9. Concentrate on the positive. When your child says,"I don't like Grandpa," sit down with him, and say, "Grandpa is part of our family. He is my father. There are things about him that I don't particularly like either, but it is our job to concentrate on the positive. Let's make a list of three things we do like about him." Even if the things you list are that he wears a blue shirt or that he smiles when the children sing songs to him, it is your job to capitalize on those things. Maybe have a singing session each time you are together. Build from there by adding some other positive qualities to your list after each visit. Your child is entitled to express his negative feelings, but he has an obligation to look for the positive.

10. Stage a **"Grandparent Appreciation Day"** every once in a while. Cook the favorite meal of the grandparent, or go to the favorite restaurant. Tell them your favorite stories about them. Reiterate how grateful you are to have a grandparent in your family.

11. Ascertain exactly what the problem is. For example, you tell your aging parent something he or she has to do the next day, and it doesn't get done. Why? Is the problem hearing loss, lack of concentration, inability to retain information, or a combination? You have to change your method of presentation. Maybe write down a schedule or a specific task that needs to be done. Make a check-off chart for his or her medication. Draw a map from his or her home to a particular store. Whatever reinforcements you use must meet your parents' needs.

12. Know when to get help. You certainly have your own set of responsibilities. The time may come when you can no longer be as available to your parents. If you feel that they are taking advantage of you or that caring for their physical or emotional needs is too much, admit it. Don't keep the resentment inside. You are entitled to feel this way, but you need to find new solutions. Perhaps you should hire a capable caregiver who will tend to the needs of your parent. Don't say you can't afford one. If the standard prices are too much for you, use your initiative and hire a neighbor to do the jobs you no

longer can or want to do. Your sanity is worth whatever price you may have to pay. You may want to consider individual counseling or other avenues of help like support groups where you can share with others your feelings about your aging parent. If there are no groups near you, start your own. Many of your friends may be feeling the same need for emotional support. If your parents do not live near you, investigate what is available in their area, or seek out geriatric counselors who specialize in working with families and aging relatives who are living apart. They assess the family needs and options and then link your aging relative to a social worker near him or her. That social worker then develops a care plan that may include regular home visits and in-home services. She also maintains frequent phone contact to all involved, aids in consultation with doctors to support medical plans, and provides crisis intervention services. Such a program offers a helping hand and a kind heart at a time when you and your parent really need help.

13. Decide what to do when your parent can no longer live by himself. Ask him what his feelings are. He probably doesn't want to be a burden to you, and he may have strong feelings about nursing homes. Some options are retirement communities, senior citizen apartment buildings, assisted living facilities, or group homes where several seniors share one home. It may be a very upsetting time for him (or her) when he has to give up his home, but he will have to realize that it is time for a different living arrangement. Be sure that the new surroundings contain as much of the old home as possible by way of decorations, photographs, or furniture. If the time comes for your parent to move to a nursing home, find one that you feel will administer care with dignity. Visit as often as you can, and be as cheerful as possible. Another alternative for some families is to have your parent move into your home. This idea can work if all parties involved live by the rules of allowing privacy, sharing responsibilities, using a sense of humor, and maintaining realistic expectations. Just as you would do when you have a concern with your children or with your colleagues, you should speak to your parent in a non-judgmental way to present a problem and garner his help to think of

a solution. He will have problems he will present to you. Remember that you are a team, a family, and you can solve whatever needs to be solved. The bestBand-Aids for emotional hurts are hugs. Dispense them regularly, and enjoy the three generational interchange.

14. Accept the cyclic nature of life. We start out as helpless, dependent babies. We do our best to achieve independence. We surround ourselves with those upon whom we want to be dependent. And often by the end of our lives, we are totally dependent again. If you have to see your aging, infirm parent being cared for like a baby, it is very difficult, but remember that this is what happens in nature. Get though the hardest times by engaging yourself in **"Five Things You Never Knew About My Parents."** Tell anyone who will listen five things you loved and five things you hated about your ailing parent. Try to understand why he or she did the ones you didn't like and how much you enjoyed the good things. Don't deny your feelings.

Eventually, you and your family will have to face death. Whether the one who dies is a grandparent, another relative, a friend, or a national figure, you should deal openly and honestly with death. You will need to do the comforting of others, and you will need to be comforted yourself. Take time for your emotional needs. Men and women, allow yourselves to cry. Crying is the way the body lets out an oversupply of emotion. Friends who want to comfort you may not know what to say, and you may not want to talk. Hugs are valuable again during these hard times. Take advantage of people's offers to help. Don't be alone. The stages of grief range from denial, anger, questioning, to depression, crying, and finally moving on.

No matter what your relationship was with your parent, there will be a void after his or her death. This void can be partially filled by sharing memories about the person. Moreover, that is the best way to explain death to your children. Whether your child is two or twenty, he probably will not be comfortable with the concept of death. A pre-schooler spends a great deal of time worrying about death. This list will be helpful to you in explaining death to your children in an honest and warm manner.

HOW TO EXPLAIN DEATH TO YOUR CHILDREN

1. Anything that is alive eventually dies.

2. People usually die when they have been very, very sick or are very, very old.

3. We don't usually know when we will die, so we have to live life to the fullest while we can.

4. When people die, they can no longer see or hear or think or talk or move. Everything stops in the person. Death is not like sleeping, because when you are asleep, you are still breathing, and you will always wake up from sleep.

5. Death is final (unless you have different religious views you wish to impart to your child).

6. When a person dies, he is put in a long box called a coffin. The coffin is closed tightly and taken to a cemetery. It is lowered into the grave, which is a long, deep hole in the ground, and is covered up with earth. During this ceremony, called a funeral, those who knew the dead person say prayers and think about him or her.

7. The rituals will differ depending on one's religious beliefs and the kind of burial accommodations chosen.

8. People show their sadness in different ways at different times. Some cry loudly often. Some keep what they feel inside of them. It is better to tell someone what you feel. It is not your fault the person died. Nothing you did could have made him or her die. It is all right if you don't feel sadness now or if you don't understand why others are sad.

9. We help ourselves through the sad times by discussing our memories about our relatives who died.

10. You may want to write down your memories about your loved one. Or you may want to donate a book to a library in his or her honor. Or you may want to keep a special picture of you and your loved one to remind you of him or her. The person may be gone, but your memories of him or her will never be.

Since death is so final, you all need to make the most out of life. Find things you can enjoy when you are in each other's company. Emphasize the positive. Remember how you wanted your freedom from your parents when you felt grown up. Give that freedom to your children when you feel the time is right.

You are the combination of what your parents have instilled in you, what you have learned on your own, and what your children have taught you. The parts from each generation form your totality. Don't de-emphasize the part that comes from your parents. In fact, elevate them in the eyes of your children and of the whole family to the position of Grand Parents. You will all benefit from doing so.

LEMON-AID

Chapter Thirteen:
Lemon-Aid

Chapter Thirteen:
Lemon-Aid

There is an old saying: "When life gives you lemons, make lemonade." Since there are many problems for which parents can use some help, some aid for the lemons of parenting life is welcome. The following are situations with which you may now or will later identify. They are based on questions I have been asked in my role as a parenting educator. By reading some of my students' questions and my answers, you may be able to pour an occasional solution to some of your problems from this chapter's pitcher of lemon-aid.

Problem #1- Mealtime- "The dinner hour in my home is torture. The baby cries during the whole meal, and the pre-schooler won't eat anything that isn't pasta. I'm afraid we'll all get ulcers."

Lemon-aid #1- First, the baby needs attention. Depending on his age, he probably doesn't have what it takes to sit at a table for the duration of an adult mealtime. So feed him when he is hungry, probably before the main dinner is ready, and let him play near the family members as they eat. To this day, and it has been a few years since I had infants, I still salivate when I hear the clicking of the indoor baby swing. We used to wind it up for a half-hour session, put the baby into it, and eat while it would click, click, click. As a result, we did have some peaceful meals in the early days.

Now that we have quieted the baby, we can turn our attention to the pre-schooler's fussiness. Because he is in his age of scientific experimentation, he will probably be more interested in eating a few items quickly and leaving the table to continue his research. Also, a pre-schooler in general just doesn't eat large portions. So if you serve him a tablespoon of each food group, it shouldn't take him very long to finish. That is, if he eats the different food groups. Children can be food specialists, eating only noodles or only peanut butter or whatever suits their appetites at any given time. Any parent who has made a fool of himself or herself trying to feed or force feed or threaten or punish a child eventually hits rock bottom. In cases like this, both you and your child have to change behaviors. Play **"Food Partners."** Explain to your child about the different food groups and why they are each important for his growing body. Tell him that you are willing to serve him one of the foods he really does like to eat, but that he has to decide which of the "partner" foods he will have for that meal. One meal his partner food must be a vegetable, the next meal a fruit, the next a starch, the next a protein. This way, he will be eating a well-rounded meal over the course of a few meals.

It is important that he have a say in the choices of the foods. Take him to the market, and let him choose which green vegetable he will eat this week. Or play **"Plan a Meal"** where he can decide what will be served during the entire meal. Or you can have him decide which seasoning can go on the chicken. Sometimes, a sprinkle of magic sauce (which adults may call paprika or cinnamon) over his "offensive" food may capture his imagination enough so that he will eat. But remember, if he does not eat a large portion, do not force him. Also, it is well within your rights to limit his "junk" food intake or the number of snacks he has between meals.

Conversations at meal time should be pleasant. Spills will happen, and since they are generally accidents, the spiller should not be punished. He does, however, have the responsibility, as soon as he is old enough, to make an attempt to clean up his spill. These spills are why we chose an apple juice-colored kitchen floor when we remodeled and why we never serve purple grape juice. Non-judgmental reminders, like "We use forks in America," will go a long way to keep meals a time during which you care to eat.

There is no law of parenting which states that you all must eat together. If you find your current situation intolerable, have two sittings for the meals. Eventually, since the children gravitate toward parental attention, they will express a desire to join your sitting. They may do so, but only if they agree to your terms of human decency at the dinner hour.

Problem #2- Dealing with Fears- "My child is afraid of robbers and fires and asks me about them every day. Will he ever stop feeling afraid?"

Lemon-aid #2- Fears are very real to your children. They struggle to understand what frightens them, and their need to understand is met by constant repetition. They may swear that the character they liked best in the story you read was the scary witch, even though they were repulsed by her. So why should they have to be exposed to these scary things? The answer is because they carry these untold frightening thoughts in their heads, and the use of witches, ghosts, and dragons gives their inner thoughts some validity. In time, they will be better able to differentiate between fact and fantasy and will feel more in control of their lives so that the fears will lessen. Soon thereafter, more realistic fears will emerge. The fears of robbers and fires exist even in adults, but we manage to keep them in proper perspective, whereas for children these fears can become a disproportionate life force. We need to tell them that the house may be robbed and that there may be a fire, but we have taken precautions which make us feel more secure. We have locks on the windows and doors and smoke detectors in proper locations. It might be helpful to your child to have him help you lock the front door at night or to help you check the smoke alarms. You cannot promise that bad things will not happen to any of you, but you can do your best to protect each other.

You should play **"I Used to be Afraid."** Tell the children about the things that caused you to feel afraid when you were small. In case you have forgotten ones you may have had, it may be necessary for you to invent a fear that someone may have, preferably one similar to the child's present fear. He will take comfort in knowing that others have felt afraid, others who have grown into adults he loves and respects.

Have practice drills about leaving the house in an emergency and about what to do if an adult becomes incapacitated. Play **"Dial an Emergency,"** by having each child dial your community's emergency number. Explain to the officer over the phone that you want your child to know what to expect if he ever had to dial in an emergency. Make certain everyone knows where to go if there is a need to leave the house quickly.

In other words, do all you can to reassure them and to educate them about frightening situations. Moreover, realize that they have to work through their fears by talking about them over and over. Even if the fears seem silly to an adult (like the fear of masks or car headlights), they are obviously something important to the child. Supply extra attention and as much explanation as you can in any given twenty-four hour period. Realize that in his quest to understand the world, he is a bit sidetracked by some of life's scary offerings. Be patient.

Problem #3- Explosive Ten Year Olds- "I can't communicate with my ten year old anymore. We used to be able to talk. I've been a responsive listener, an open and approachable parent all these years, and now all our conversations end in explosion. What happened to my formerly pleasant child? Why is he so unhappy?"

Lemon-aid #3- Your formerly pleasant child is in a stage of development that is harder for him than it is for you. In his striving to become independent, to move away from the family circle, he needs to stand on his own two feet. And when those two feet come stomping down, it doesn't matter who gets hurt under them. He is looking for his own values and needs to make some of his own mistakes. This scenario is harder to live through when the child is sixteen, because at the pre-teen level, he is still willing to be independent one minute and completely dependent and sorry the next. The pre-teen is undergoing physical changes and emotional traumas. One minute he'll want to share his life with you. The next minute his thoughts are completely sealed inside. He runs hot or cold, friend or enemy. Your job is to stand back during the enemy phase and be there when he needs you to be on his side.

As much as you have no control over his feelings, you do have the responsibility to set limits on his actions. His behavior must remain within your family guidelines. He will also need, during this painful period, reassurance that every child has these feelings. When he was younger, he may have felt support from books, like the stories of the Berenstain Bears or the Care Bears. Now some more mature bibliotherapy will be helpful. He also needs to realize that it is common for children to have compulsions. He may have thought he was the only one in the world who had to tap his window three times before going to sleep or who had to touch his heel on every other step on the staircase. These compulsions, as long as they don't dominate his actions, can be the normal reactions he has to his "bad" feelings. He may feel he must punish himself for this anger against his parents or for his other antisocial thoughts. His punishment often takes the form of making strict rules of behavior for himself. While these compulsions are at their strongest, your child needs added reassurance from you that what he is experiencing is normal and that the intensity of the compulsions will lessen and eventually disappear as he develops further.

No one said it was easy to grow up, but if you can savor the moments when he is not your "enemy," you will see a sparkle of the child you used to know and a glimmer of hope that you will want to live with him again in the future.

Problem #4- Adoption, Illness, Divorce- "I just found out that my neighbor's child is adopted, my uncle had a heart attack, and my cousins are getting a divorce. What do I tell the children?"

Lemon-aid #4- You tell them as much as you think they can understand, depending on their age. You can't go wrong by being honest, even if what you are explaining is surprising, startling, or bad news.

Your child will probably first want to know if any of the upsetting or bad things will ever happen to him. Or if you are explaining some upsetting situation in your own family, he will want to know what will happen to those most affected.

About adoption– his friend is very fortunate to be with people who want him for their child. He will have all the loving from his adopted parents, and it shouldn't make any difference in our relationship with him.

With a heart attack or any other serious illness, the child should be told that he is not to blame for the person becoming ill. The sick person will need to have the family around him to help in his recovery. If death is imminent, the child should be told what to expect. He should see adults grieve openly, and he should be encouraged to tell you how he feels, no matter what those feelings are.

Divorce affects the child deeply. He needs to understand that the parents have divorced each other, but they can never divorce the child. The child of the divorcing couple may think that he is the cause of the break-up or that if he would only do something, his parents would live happily ever after, together with him. You don't need to explain all the personal details of the divorce, but it is your responsibility to help your child understand the situation.

If your child is troubled about hearing that someone he knows is getting a divorce, he also needs reassurance. Tell him what he can expect with his own parents. Nothing is ever definite, but what do you think will probably happen? And will you ever stop loving him, even if you stop loving his other parent?

All of life's traumas affect your child. He may create scenarios in his head that are much worse than the reality of the situation. So be as honest as you can, and be available to him when he needs to unload emotionally.

Problem #5- Peer Pressure- "I feel like a terrible parent. In fact, I'm often told that I am by my own child, because I don't let him do all the things the other children are allowed to do."

Lemon-aid #5- The problem of peer pressure grows in relation to the child's age. At first, the new parent tries to "keep up with" the activities of other people's babies or nursery triumphs, and the child is probably not at all interested in competing. Then as the child matures, he becomes more interested in being part of the group, doing what is the "in" thing to do. Finally, peer pressure reaches its zenith (or nadir, depending on whether you are the parent or the teenager) when the child is in high school.

There are times when you should allow your child to give in to peer pressure. Certain fad clothes are a good example. You can probably sell your child on the merits of a sensible wardrobe much better if you add to it a few items that are the latest fad. It really is important for the child to feel as though he belongs.

But you need to know where to set limits. "Peer" pressure has always reminded me of its homonym, "pier" pressure. It is like walking to the end of the pier. If you are not properly anchored to that pier, you are in danger of falling into the deep. What anchors you are standards. You need family standards and personal standards. Then you can comfortably say, "Different families have different lifestyles and different religious celebrations. We can learn about what they do, but we might not allow some of those things to be done by our family members."

You are the parent and so are entitled to set the standards for your family. Of course, it never hurts to listen to what the children have to say or to bend the rules some of the time. But if you feel comfortable about your standards, you have the obligation to uphold them.

Problem #6- Toys- "My children want every toy they see advertised. When I do go into a toy store, I feel overwhelmed at the enormous selection. I never know what to buy, and, deep down, I question the value of toys altogether."

Lemon-aid #6- Good toys have a good purpose. They stimulate

the senses of the baby, excite the imagination of the middle-aged child, and expand the mind of the older child. Actually, they should entertain all of us at any age. A good toy is one that is sturdy, safe, and interesting for its age group. The best toys are those which are run by child power, whether physical or mental. Crayons, blocks, puzzles, balls, dolls, and action figures don't come with a set of directions. They are meant to be used in any way one wants. When you can think of six games to play with one eighteen inch piece of ribbon, you are employing your creative powers wonderfully. When should you give in to advertising pressure or "begging-from-the-children" pressure? Sometimes, but usually you can say, "I'm willing to look at the toy in the store to see if it is worth the money." Every once in a while it is a good value lesson to buy the toy the child can definitely not live without. When he brings it to you in pieces or when he realizes that it really doesn't work the way it did in the commercial, you can point out the wisdom of being a more experienced consumer. There are times when he needs tangible evidence that "all that glitters is not gold."

When you need to go into a toy store, so as not to feel overwhelmed, you need to have a game plan. Play **"Toy Store Attack."** Attack the store by age category. Not sex, but age. When you stand in front of the counter of the age-appropriate toys, you are actually having to deal with a smaller section rather than the entire store. If you are fortunate enough to be standing near a more experienced toy shopper, ask his or her help. "Which toy would you recommend?" "What is wrong with this one?" If you hear an answer like "too many pieces," and the toy is for your home, you may not want to buy it.

If you happen to be escorting a child into a toy store, you may want to set down some rules before both of you enter the store. Purpose of visit, amount to be spent, number of minutes allowed in the store are important discussion points. Often, when your children find that they are allowed to spend all their birthday money, they will eye everything, but then they will study the price tags. Remember, if it is their money, they should be allowed to spend it on anything they like. Weapon toys may be your only exception. If you are morally opposed to having guns in your home, make your feelings clear. However, just because the guns may not physically be in the house, there is always the carrot, which after several key bites have been taken, looks like a gun. Children will play out their aggressions with pretend objects or real ones. You cannot stop what is in their imagination. You can only suggest alternative outlets.

Comments like "We can't afford that toy" and "We aren't going to buy anything now" are perfectly acceptable for parents to make. You should also store one-third of your toy collection every few months. By rotating your stock, you will see that the children view the "newly released" ones as almost new. Also, before a holiday or a birthday, you may want to play **"Select for Giving,"** whereby your child decides which toys he is ready to pass along to charity for those in greater need.

Problem #7- Censorship- "I don't want my child to see sex and violence on TV, on the computer, or at the movies, and I don't even know what is in the books he reads."

Lemon-aid #7- The whole idea of censorship has to be age appropriate. When your child is quite young, you obviously can exert control over what he watches and what he reads. You can monitor his TV and computer and take him only to those movies about which you feel comfortable. However, as he gets older, your control diminishes. As for TV, you can reinforce your value system by discussing the themes of the programs. As for the movies, especially when your teens start going to them on their own, you should also reinforce your morality. For example, you can explain how the violence on the screen lessens the value of a human life and, therefore, lessens humanity. Sex on the screen can be handled in a beautiful way or in a degrading way. Of course, by the time they have reached this teenage stage, you have already discussed that sex is wonderful, but not until the time is right. In regard to books, you really don't know what is within the covers unless you have read the book yourself, and that plan might not be very practical. Teenagers will probably read whatever they want, and sometimes we should be grateful that at least they are reading something. So as long as they understand what values you hold dear, they should be allowed to read or view just about anything. With your guidance, they will develop their own value system with their own morality. This system may be the same as yours, or it may be different. Thereafter, they will be able to see how the literature or the entertainment can fit into their value system. You will need to respect them for their lifestyles, just as you want them to respect you for yours. This is how the generations will get along, by mutual respect.

Problem #8- Moods- "I can't stand the mood swings in my family. As soon as one child has calmed down from a tantrum, another one starts to be crabby. It is almost like 'tag-team tantrums.'"

Lemon-aid #8- If only everyone could be in a good mood at the same time and a bad mood at the same time, life would be much easier. By the time the children are back in good spirits, the parents are often so drained that they don't want to be near humans for a long time. But we have to remember that children are children. They don't have the adult controls for their behavior and shouldn't have to have them. They need to be accepted for what they are– moody, changeable, flexible, and inflexible. They can't live in a family where they have to take a number like in a bakery to have a scheduled crabby period. Therefore, we must not become so involved in their bad moods. We certainly should avoid getting into power struggles with them. When they are having a tantrum, we remove them or ourselves until they can regain their control.

Keep in mind that adults have mood swings also. Perhaps problems at work, either inside the home or outside the home, have been disturbing. Maybe you have monthly mood swings according to your hormone levels. Or you may experience daily mood swings depending on how tired you are or on how the children have been behaving. The bottom line is that you must be understanding when it is most needed. If someone is in a bad mood, wait awhile. Like the weather, it will change. Play **"Press Your Pleasant Button."** Find the person's imaginary pleasant button, and press it to help him have a mood change. Likewise, finding a ticklish spot always makes it easier.

When you have tried to ignore the children, tried to be as understanding as you can about your spouse's moods, and you still aren't happy with what is going on around you, then play **"I'm Going to Change This."** Change the scene by taking the family out for a ride or a walk or a game of catch in the back yard. Change the mood by doing something completely unpredictable like putting everyone in the shower with their clothes on or starting to cook some messy recipe. Redirect their energies, and give large doses of positive reinforcement when they are in good moods.

Problem #9- Independence- "I want my child to be independent, but he is only a child. How do I know when to let go at each step in his development?"

Lemon-aid #9- The cure for the problem of independence versus dependence lies in taking the cue from your child. Actually, he has been directing you all along. When he was very young, he was the one who told you when he was hungry or tired or wet. You took your cues from him then. When he was ready to walk on his own, you knew when to let go of his hand, because he let you know. When he was in the process of becoming toilet trained, you took cues from him. When he was ready to put sounds together to begin reading, you helped him. All along, he has been guiding you to be a good parent.

The trouble develops when he feels ready to do something about which you are uncomfortable. It may be crossing a street by himself, going to a sleepover, or attending a dance party. After you have said "no" to one of his requests and have been inundated by his incredibly advanced debating skills, play **"Stand Back."** This game asks you to stand back to think of the worst things that could happen in regard to his request. If the answer is that he might get hit by a car, then you have to work on his safety skills. If the answer is that your teen might start to engage in sexual activities at too early an age, then you need to explain your worry and your value system. You acquiesce when his argument makes more sense than yours does.

179

However, if the worst thing that could happen is that he might not get enough sleep or that he will be doing something without your supervision, then maybe you should give in to his persuasive arguments. His self-esteem will be enhanced, especially if he returns from the market without a mishap or if he finishes cooking the dinner all by himself. It is your job to oversee the development of your children. That overseeing must be a healthy combination of imposing your standards and taking cues from him. No matter what your ages, you all need room to breathe, to grow, to get along together.

Problem #10- Carpools- "My child is in a carpool with a driver who is inconsiderate. She doesn't let me know when she will be late, and her child is never ready on time."

Lemon-aid #10- Life in the suburbs often dictates the need for carpools. So carpool etiquette becomes important. You need to deal courteously with those involved and discuss openly with them anything that bothers you.

If you are the driver, you must provide a safe car that has seat belts for each passenger. You must arrive on time for pick-up and drop-off. You must obey the traffic laws. Everyone wants to follow these rules, but unforeseen circumstances are bound to occur. So if your car breaks down, know whom to call. Have the names of the other drivers with you in case of an emergency. When you find that you will be late or cannot drive at all, it is up to you to make other arrangements. It is also up to you to have the courtesy to apologize to the other parents whenever you do not or cannot live up to your part of the carpool agreement.

If you are the parent of the child who will be picked up, you must be certain that he is ready before the scheduled pick-up time. That means jackets on and zipped before the car arrives. You should discuss his car manners and make an arrangement with the other drivers that you will all remind each other about schedule changes. You need each other, so the most important thing to remember about carpool etiquette is that you all should be thoughtful and courteous.

Problem #11- Overreacting- "I think I worry too much about my child's safety and health. Maybe I call the doctor too much with questions. How do I know if I am overreacting?"

Lemon-aid #11- Because you are caring, involved parents, you want the best for your children. Your guide for determining if you are overreacting is that if you think you are, you probably are. Parents tend to overreact or call the doctor often or inhibit their child's actions because the parents feel insecure. The best counter-force to your insecurity is to trust your own judgments and your own instincts. You can ask three authorities about your problem, and you may receive four solutions, none of which may really work. The best course of action is for you to learn all you can about your problem, listen to those around you, and then make your own decision. Unless something happens to make you change your mind, follow your instincts. Then you can feel secure knowing you have done the right thing.

Generally, if people tell you that you are overreacting, you probably are. You need to team up with a more experienced parent, an understanding doctor, a concerned parenting educator, or, in the case of a major problem, a support group of those who have been through such problems. Express your concerns to someone whose opinions you trust. In parenting, often after you have faced a problem, you then become the expert, and others turn to you for advice. I remember when my first child was three days old, a friend, whose baby was only one day old, called me for advice about nursing him. Now that is about as weak a definition of expert as I can imagine! The point is that you want to feel secure about your parenting decisions so that you run a better, more relaxed household.

Problem #12- Excuses- "Often, when I tell my child he has done something wrong, he gives an excuse and thinks that is enough. What can I do to point out the error of his ways?"

Lemon-aid #12- A frequent problem is that of dealing with a child's excuses. When a child engages in misbehavior, like acting irresponsibly or failing to do a chore, he will often offer an excuse.

Your task is to decide how to deal with that excuse. Excuses can fall into two groups: those that are acceptable and those that are not. The first group is the smaller one by far. It includes cases where there were valid reasons for not doing the proper thing. For example, the dog really did chew up the slipper, or Grandma kept him on the phone well into his chore time. The second group is the bigger and more diverse one. It includes cases where the child blames a sibling unfairly or argues that the assignment was too difficult in the first place or blames you for demanding too much of him. Your job is to listen carefully, with an open mind, and to decide if the child might have a valid point. Remember that a child often cannot articulate the real reason for his concern. If the excuse is a "good" one, relent. If the excuse is unacceptable, tell him that, and explain why. In any event, listen to your child carefully, explain your reaction, and lead him onto the proper path of behavior.

Problem #13- Language Development- "My first child was very advanced in language development. But my second child doesn't talk much at all, and he is already almost three years old. What did I do wrong? Will my younger one ever be normal?"

Lemon-aid #13- Just as they walk at different times, children begin to talk at different times. The age span for what is still considered normal development is quite wide. And as the old expression goes, "You can lead a horse to water, but you can't make him drink." You can speak to a child, provide him with a stimulating environment, praise his smallest utterances, and he still may not speak. But, unless there is some physical or mental problem, he will speak when he is ready. Remember how you went into labor when he was ready?

If, at any time, you feel concerned about his development, you should have a speech specialist test him. If therapy or remedial work is indicated, then begin it with a good attitude that it will be helpful to your child. But, if there are no physical problems, relax. He will speak when he is ready. There is a joke that may make you feel better if your child is slower than you would like him to be in his speech development. "A child from a warm, loving home had never spoken. His third birthday passed, his fourth, his fifth, but still no words came out of his mouth. His parents were beside themselves with worry. One day, during dinner, the child suddenly said, 'The soup is cold.' His parents looked at each other in astonishment. Then the father asked him, 'Why didn't you speak before this?' The child answered, 'Everything was all right up until now!'"

To provide a stimulating language environment for your child, you need to speak well yourselves. Practice good grammar. Avoid the common mistakes. Some proper usages are: "He feels bad." "It is really exciting." "This is she." You are your child's best English teacher. Never speak down to him. Enlarge his vocabulary by exposing him to the beauty of words. Some of my favorite expressions I have used in front of my two-year-olds are:

1. Tell me in words.
2. Get it in your head before you speak.
3. That is unacceptable.
4. This is appropriate.
5. Here is our schedule.
6. This is your responsibility.

My children have large vocabularies, because we have talked to them as we would talk to adults. Of course, there are many times when a less sophisticated word works well. My favorite multi-purpose negative word is "yucky," or if something is really bad, I use "yuck-and-a-half." Don't forget the advantages of exposing them to other languages at an early age. Your children reflect how you speak, and they will begin when they are good and ready.

Problem #14- No Longer An Authority Figure- "I am no longer an authority figure for my teenager. He feels I don't understand him, and he is probably right."

Lemon-aid #14- Parents remain authority figures for only a small part of their parenting careers. It is the job of the teenager to move away emotionally from the parents, to forge ahead on his own. He needs you there as a compass for his course of maturation, but there will come a point when he will want to cut the childhood ties and be on his own. He may only be fifteen and still living at home when he may rebel against authority. This is painful for all involved, but if you remember that it is not personal, but professional (since his job is to be a maturing person), you can live with it better.

When he says that you don't understand his life or him or his clothes, play **"Teach Me."** Tell him you really do want to understand how he feels about things. Have him make a list of five things that are important to him. Listen to three of his records. Meet two of his friends. As you make this effort to understand about him at this stage of his life, he will appreciate your concern and may not feel so threatened about you and about growing up, which can be a very scary process.

Think of the rebellious teenage years as a driver education car, the kind with the two steering wheels. Your teenager is in the driver's seat steering his own way through these years. You are seated next to him with your emergency steering wheel ready to be used in case he goes too far off the road. Give him credit for being a good driver of his life, and be comfortable knowing that you are there when he needs you.

Problem #15- Setting Limits- "I don't know when to say 'no' to my toddler, and then there are times when I think that I restrict him too much. I am confused about how to set limits."

Lemon-aid #15- Setting limits is a hard part of the parenting job. At first, we think that our children should have everything, that nothing should be denied to them. For an infant, of course, this is true. He can't be spoiled by your responding to his physical needs. For a toddler, however, that is not how the real world works. We have to teach him what are acceptable standards for behavior. He will come to look to you for guidance and, paradoxically, ignore many things that you say. But it is your responsibility to say the "no" when it is appropriate. If you find that you are being negative a great deal of the time, you will be able to parent better by focusing on the positive side. Instead of "Do not stand on the chair," you should rephrase your command to something like "Chairs are for sitting." When he reaches the rebellious stages, you are better off keeping your negatives for the very serious transgressions. Some important phrases for you in setting limits are "I can't allow you to do that." "I will be happy to speak to you when your crying has stopped." "We will be leaving in five more minutes." "You are out of control. Let me know when you feel better." "Do you want to go to bed in three minutes or in four minutes?" The more children understand about what will be happening to them, the more cooperative they may be (although there are many other factors of moods and developmental levels to consider). But it doesn't hurt for you to explain what his behavioral limits are and then uphold your standards.

Sometimes, you can use the help of an outside authority figure. When my daughter refused at age two to wear her mittens during the winter, I made use of the TV weatherman's warnings. I told her that Weatherman Bob said that it will be so cold that all children should be bundled up. She was impressed that someone other than her parent could give her advice, and she wore her mittens from then on.

You are the parent, and therefore you have the right to limit behavior, such as aggression and discourtesy. You and your spouse may have to caucus to decide what limits you should set. But once you have decided, be strong. Your child can only benefit from your good and consistent discipline.

Problem #16- Single Parenting- "I am a single parent and find that I am overwhelmed because of all the things I must do. I am afraid that my children will suffer."

Lemon-aid #16- The most ideal parenting, that with a mother and a father living together, is oftentimes difficult and overwhelming. Since, for whatever reason, you are parenting by yourself, you are probably not receiving emotional support and relief from another interested adult. Relief for you may come in the form of the game **"Listening Partner."** You need to ask a relative, friend, or professional to function formally as your listening partner. Speak to this person almost daily. Tell him or her the three best things and the three worst things that happened to you as a parent that day. Listen for the feedback and the support. You need suggestions and praise for what you are doing. You also should hire help in whatever area you need. The cost is an investment in your mental health.

Further, to feel less overwhelmed, be sure you are as organized as you can be. Make lists, plan well in advance, and find people to be your back-up support for unforeseeable circumstances. Schedule into your week some time for you to do something just for yourself.

As to whether or not the children will suffer, be certain you have a large supply of the **"Three L's."** They are love, listening, and leadership. Your children will thrive because you give to them unlimited love, careful listening, and wise leadership from you and other respected adults. With the **"Three L's,"** your family unit will be united in excellence.

Problem #17- Sexual Identification- "I worry that if my son plays with dolls and my daughter likes sports, they will have trouble with their sexual identification. Should I restrict their play?"

Lemon-aid #17- Current research says that sexual identification has both a biological and an environmental genesis. Your children shape their behavior, in the beginning, on the basis of their role models. If the mother and the father are in the home, the child can observe how both sexes behave. If the home has a single parent, you must allow your child to be around an adult of the opposite sex, whether it be a friend, a relative, or someone in a Big Brother– or Big Sister–type program.

During their Oedipal or Electra stage, when children fantasize about killing the opposite sex parent and marrying the same sex parent, they are working through, in their subconscious minds and very often through dreams with couched meanings, who they are and what they are capable of doing. As long as they have healthy sexual models in the parents, they will thrive in their identification no matter what their play entails. Boys should play with dolls for the same reason girls should. They need to practice their home skills and their parenting skills and show their love for their toys. The more they practice and feel secure in showing their feelings, the better fathers, the better people, they will become. Likewise, girls should be encouraged to join in sports for the same reasons boys do. They need the physical outlets and the channeling of their aggression. Sound minds and healthy bodies make strong boys and girls.

Similarly, no chore is a girl's chore or a boy's chore. If a job needs to be done, either sex can do it and should do it. Non-sexist child rearing makes well-rounded children into well-rounded adults and future parents.

After the working through of their Oedipal or Electra stages, they turn their psyches to identifying with the same sex parent. During this elementary school age, children mainly befriend their same sex child. But by about age thirteen, their identification shifts from their parents to their idols. As they search for their adolescent identities, they model their behavior, both positive and negative, on television or movie stars, teachers, and friends. This way is one means by which they learn how to relate to other adults. During this time when they need us and they don't want us at the same time, they are working psychologically to complete their identities. From the sound basis of modeling you have laid for them and from their biological predetermination, whatever that may be, they will blossom. The best course of your action is to give them a grounding in moral standards and accept the conclusions they reach after their difficult emergence from their adolescent cocoons.

Problem #18- Transitions- "I don't want to let go of my baby. I hated it when I had to take him to the first day of school, and I certainly will never be able to allow him to move away from home no matter how old he gets!"

Lemon-aid #18- Sometimes it is difficult to know if life's transitions are harder for the parent or the child. The milestones we face should be met head on. Parents must be allowed the luxury of wallowing in the poignancy of the moment. Today is his first time away from home or his first day of school or his first date. These are what memories are all about. What is a positive step for him is often a difficult step for parents. But we must let go when the time dictates. Remember the two greatest gifts you are giving him– roots and wings. Console yourselves with photographs, saved arts and crafts, and mementos, and store treasured words or actions in notebooks or in your memories.

Problem #19- Doing the Right Thing- "How do I know if I am doing the right thing for my child? What if I make a mistake?"

Lemon-aid #19- No parent can be perfect. We all make mistakes and learn from them. It is all right to make mistakes. We develop as they grow.

When your child is very young and you are not confident about your parenting, learn to trust your instincts, ask for advice, or seek professional help. When your child gets older and you are not sure if you are doing the right things for him, you can continue to ask for advice, but you can also ask your child. Play **"Strengths and Weaknesses."** Have him make a list of your good parenting points and your bad ones. Discuss each point in a non-defensive manner. You do not have to change anything you do, but you may want to after seeing how your child views your actions.

Whenever the time comes for us to change our tactics, all we have to do is admit we were wrong and decide to start again. Life is more easily lived if you can change direction smoothly. Children adapt easily and often. Frequently, they can lead us. We should follow their example and their flexibility. When you feel comfortable about your parent-child relationship, then you are doing a good job and all your family members are indeed fortunate.

Conclusion

Conclusion

Through the games and other suggestions in this book, I have guided you toward making the most of your parenting instincts and making your daily situations more pleasant. The concept of pleasant parenting is admirable, but what if you don't feel like being pleasant? Certainly, there are times when you feel miserable, and the cause of your mood is often due to something the children did. You now have two choices. You can continue to have a bad day, or you can do something positive, something to make the situation pleasant.

Why do you have to accept a less than ideal lifestyle, perhaps lower your standards, to raise your children? The answer that you may need to repeat at hard moments is that doing so elevates you as a person, because it enriches you as a parent who will be more tolerant of your child's developmental levels.

Your time as a parent who has total controlling influence is short because you really don't have your children for too many years. So you might as well make the best of what you have. Every once in a while, you should step back from the scene, as the girl did in Thornton Wilder's play *Our Town*. When she was in a position to view her life as an observer, she wondered if anyone really appreciated life during the day-to-day living. When you do observe your scene, appreciate it. This is your family, and it is wonderful.

Being pleasant means being positive, optimistic, and fun loving.

Look for the good, the joy, the love. Be your own family's magician who can turn the parenting lemons into lemonade.

In any family situation, the bad times are inevitable, so make them pass quickly by thinking of more pleasant times or more pleasant ways to handle the situation. In fact, this brings us to the last game in this book. Play **"List your Pleasant Memories."** Write down what each family member feels is a pleasant memory about your life together. Do all you can in the future to add to that list.

Treat your children respectfully, remembering that children should behave like children. Guide them to become pleasant parents when their time comes. Take comfort in this old saying: "Parents hold their children's hands for a little while, their hearts forever."

Bibliography

1. Ames, Louise Bates, and Carol Chase Haber, *He Hit Me First: When Brothers and Sisters Fight*, New York, Dembner Books, 1982.

2. Beck, Joan, *How to Raise a Brighter Child*, New York, Trident Press, 1967.

3. Brazelton, T. Berry, *Infants and Mothers: Differences in Development*, New York, Delacorte, 1973.

4. Brazelton, T. Berry, *Toddlers and Parents: A Declaration of Independence*, New York, Dell Publishing Company, 1974.

5. Briggs, Dorothy C., *Your Child's Self-Esteem*, New York, Doubleday and Company, Inc., 1970.

6. Caplan, Frank, Editor, *Parents' Yellow Pages*, New York, Doubleday, 1978.

7. Dodson, Fitzhugh, *How to Parent*, New York, New American Library, 1970.

8. Dreikurs, Rudolf, *Children: The Challenge*, New York, Dutton, 1964.

9. Editors of *Better Homes and Gardens*, *Better Homes and Gardens Baby Book*, New York, Bantam Books, 1974.

10. Elkins, David, *The Hurried Child: Growing Up Too Fast Too Soon*, Reading, Massachusetts, Addison-Wesley, 1981.

11. Engelmann, Siegfried and Therese, *Give Your Child a Superior Mind*, New York, Simon and Schuster, 1966.

12. Forer, Lucille K., *Birth Order and Life Roles*, New York, C.C. Thomas, 1969.

13. Fraiberg, Selma H., *The Magic Years*, New York, Charles Scribner's Sons, 1959.

14. Freed, Alvyn, *T.A. for Tots*, Sacramento, California, Jalmar, 1973.

15. Friday, Nancy, *My Mother Myself*, New York, Dell, 1981.

16. Galton, Lawrence, *Don't Give Up on an Aging Parent*, New York, Crown Publishers, Inc., 1975.

17. Gesell, Arnold and Frances Ilg and Louise Ames, *Youth*, New York, Harper and Row, 1956.

18. Ginott, Haim, *Between Parent and Child*, New York, Avon, 1973.

19. Gordon, Thomas, *P.E.T.- Parent Effectiveness Training*, New York, Wyden, 1970.

20. Gregg, Elizabeth and Boston Children's Medical Center, *What to Do When There is Nothing to Do*, New York, Dell, 1984.

21. Harris, Thomas, *I'm OK, You're OK*, New York, Avon, 1967.

22. Ilg, Frances L. and Louise B. Ames, *Child Behavior*, New York, Barnes and Noble, 1982.

23. James, Muriel and Dorothy Jongward, *Born to Win: Transactional Analysis with Gestalt Experiment*, Reading, Massachusetts, Addison-Wesley Publishing Company, 1971.

24. James, Muriel, *What Do You Do With Them Now That You've Got Them?*, Reading, Massachusetts, Addison-Wesley, 1974.

25. Kelly, Marguerite and Elia S. Parsons, *Mother's Almanac*, New York, Doubleday, 1975.

26. Mark, Allison, *Toilet Learning*, New York, Little Brown, 1978.

27. Marzollo, Jean and Janice Lloyd, *Learning Through Play*, New York, Harper and Row, 1974.

28. Morris, Desmond, *The Naked Ape*, New York, Dell, 1984.

29. Moyer, Inez D., *Responding to Infants: The Infant Activity Manual*, Minneapolis, Minnesota, T.S. Denison and Company, Inc., 1983.

30. Neill, A.S., *Summerhill: A Radical Approach to Child Rearing*, New York, Hart, 1966.

31. Otten, Jane and Florence D. Shelley, *When Your Parents Grow Old*, New York, Funk and Wagnalls, 1976.

32. Pogrebin, Letty, *Family Politics, Love and Power on an Intimate Frontier*, New York, McGraw, 1983.

33. Pogrebin, Letty. *Growing Up Free*, New York, Bantam, 1981.

34. Rivers, Caryl, and Rosalind Barnett and Grace Baruch, *Beyond Sugar and Spice: How Women Grow, Learn, and Thrive*, New York, G.P. Putnam's Sons, 1979.

35. Satir, Virginia, *Peoplemaking*, Palo Alto, California, Science and Behavior Books, Inc., 1972.

36. Sheehy, Gail, *Passages*, New York, Bantam, 1977.

37. Spock, Benjamin, *Baby and Child Care*, New York, Pocket Books, 1974.

38. Stone, L. Joseph and Joseph Church, *Childhood and Adolescence*, New York, Random House, 1984.

39. White, Burton, *A Parent's Guide to the First Three Years of Life*, New Jersey, Prentice Hall, 1980.

Printed in the United States
20265LVS00008B/40-42